Learning BeagleBone Python Programming

Unleash the potential of BeagleBone using Python

Alexander Hiam

PUBLISHING

BIRMINGHAM - MUMBAI

Learning BeagleBone Python Programming

First published: July 2015

Production reference: 1080715

Published by Packt Publishing Ltd.
Livery Place
35 Livery Street
Birmingham B3 2PB, UK.

ISBN 978-1-78439-970-2

www.packtpub.com

Credits

Author
Alexander Hiam

Reviewers
Pete Bachant

Hardik Vijaykumar Pandya

Acquisition Editor
Shaon Basu

Content Development Editor
Anand Singh

Technical Editor
Bharat Patil

Copy Editor
Merilyn Pereira

Project Coordinator
Vijay Kushlani

Proofreader
Safis Editing

Indexer
Rekha Nair

Production Coordinator
Aparna Bhagat

Cover Work
Aparna Bhagat

About the Author

Alexander Hiam is a freelance embedded systems designer. He has a bachelor's degree in computer science (embedded systems) from Marlboro College. He is the sole proprietor of Gray Cat Labs, where he has been doing contract software and hardware development since 2012.

Alex developed and actively maintains the PyBBIO Python library for BeagleBone. He has designed BeagleBone Capes professionally for clients, and he also actively contributes to the BeagleBone community by helping provide support on the mailing list and IRC channel and mentoring for the BeagleBoard.org organization during Google Summer of Code.

> I'd like to thank my cat, Moondog, for being so patient with me while I worked on this book, as he was sure I should have been playing with him instead.

About the Reviewers

Pete Bachant is a mechanical engineering PhD student at the University of New Hampshire who enjoys writing Python and uses the BeagleBone to interact with motion control and data acquisition hardware.

Hardik Vijaykumar Pandya is an electrical engineering graduate from TU Delft in the Netherlands. He's been working on open source hardware and software for the last 7 years and has conducted state-wide workshops on them in different universities across Gujarat, India.

His projects have been selected for display at the national level and his work on hobby electronics has been lauded by the mayor of Ahmedabad a number of times. His work on optical shape and motion recognition using the Microsoft Kinect camera also won the best and most innovative project of the year award at Nirma University.

Nowadays, he reviews books on subjects related to electronics and manages his own business in the same domain. He does a lot of public speaking on the topics of getting started with electronics and entrepreneurship. He also writes articles at `http://hardik.org` and shares his views on Twitter. His Twitter handle is `@hvpandya`.

He can be reached for questions and queries at `hardik@hardik.org`.

www.PacktPub.com

Support files, eBooks, discount offers, and more

For support files and downloads related to your book, please visit www.PacktPub.com.

Did you know that Packt offers eBook versions of every book published, with PDF and ePub files available? You can upgrade to the eBook version at www.PacktPub.com and as a print book customer, you are entitled to a discount on the eBook copy. Get in touch with us at service@packtpub.com for more details.

At www.PacktPub.com, you can also read a collection of free technical articles, sign up for a range of free newsletters and receive exclusive discounts and offers on Packt books and eBooks.

https://www2.packtpub.com/books/subscription/packtlib

Do you need instant solutions to your IT questions? PacktLib is Packt's online digital book library. Here, you can search, access, and read Packt's entire library of books.

Why subscribe?

- Fully searchable across every book published by Packt
- Copy and paste, print, and bookmark content
- On demand and accessible via a web browser

Free access for Packt account holders

If you have an account with Packt at www.PacktPub.com, you can use this to access PacktLib today and view 9 entirely free books. Simply use your login credentials for immediate access.

Table of Contents

Preface   **v**

Chapter 1: Before We Begin   **1**

An overview of BeagleBone   **1**
  General purpose input/output   2
  Analog-to-digital converter   3
Pulse width modulation   **4**
  Universal asynchronous receiver/transmitter   4
  Serial peripheral interface   5
  Inter-Integrated Circuit   6
Tools and additional hardware   **6**
The BeagleBone design   **8**
Board comparison   **9**
Helpful resources   **10**
Summary   **10**

Chapter 2: Getting Started   **11**

Initial setup   **11**
Updating your Debian image   **12**
Connecting to your BeagleBone   **14**
  The Cloud9 IDE   14
  SSH   15
Connecting to the Internet   **17**
  Ethernet   17
  Network forwarding   18
Using the serial console   **22**
Updating your software   **23**
The PyBBIO library   **23**
The Adafruit_BBIO library   **25**
Summary   **26**

Chapter 3: Digital Outputs — 27

GPIO modules — 27
  Kernel drivers — 27
  Pin multiplexing — 28
Interactive GPIO — 29
Calculating resistor values for LEDs — 32
Driving higher currents from GPIO pins — 33
Blink — 36
Taking advantage of the OS — 36
  Multiprocessing — 37
  Running at startup — 38
Summary — 39

Chapter 4: PWM and ADC Subsystems — 41

PWM — 41
  Fading an LED — 44
  Servo motors — 45
ADC — 49
  Voltage divider — 49
  Voltage follower — 51
Your first robot — 55
Summary — 58

Chapter 5: User Input — 59

Buttons — 59
  Pull-up/pull-down resistors — 61
  Polling — 63
  Interrupts — 70
Potentiometers — 72
Summary — 76

Chapter 6: Program Output — 77

LED displays — 77
  LED bar graphs — 80
  7-segment displays — 82
  The LED matrix — 85
SMTP — 87
Character LCD — 90
Summary — 93

Chapter 7: Serial Communication — 95

Serial communication — 95
UART — 95
I2C — 104
SPI — 110
Summary — 115

Chapter 8: Interfacing with External Devices — 117

Accelerometers — 117
  Hooking it up — 118
  Reading data — 119
  Writing a module — 121
  Using interrupts — 124
Summary — 132

Chapter 9: Using the Network — 133

TCP/IP — 133
HTTP — 139
IoT Services — 141
  Phant — 141
  dweet.io — 144
  Freeboard — 147
Summary — 152

Chapter 10: A Practical Example — 153

Weather station — 153
Connecting to the Internet — 155
Weather alerts — 159
Summary — 167

Appendix A: The BeagleBone Black Pinout — 169

Appendix B: Disabling HDMI — 171

Index — 173

Preface

The BeagleBone Black is a powerful system that can be used in a huge number of cool projects and is a great platform to learn about embedded systems and embedded Linux, but it can be difficult for beginners to find the resources they need to get started with it. The goal of this book is to use the Python programming language to introduce you to many of the different hardware interfaces available on the BeagleBone Black, and to teach you how to use them to communicate with external hardware with the help of the PyBBIO and Adafruit_BBIO Python libraries. This book will take you through the system, from initial setup to creating complete programs, and each new concept along the way is introduced with practical and contextual examples.

What this book covers

Chapter 1, *Before We Begin*, introduces you to the BeagleBone Black and to each of its hardware interfaces that are used throughout the book.

Chapter 2, *Getting Started*, takes you through the initial steps to get your BeagleBone Black setup and ready to use, and briefly introduces you to the PyBBIO and Adafruit_BBIO Python libraries.

Chapter 3, *Digital Outputs*, goes more in depth into using the GPIO modules to generate digital outputs, and guides you through your first hardware interface programs to blink some LEDs.

Chapter 4, *PWM and ADC Subsystems*, describes in more detail the pulse width modulation and analog-to-digital converter subsystems, and guides you through using them to fade LEDs, control servo motors, measure light levels, and more. It also introduces some basic concepts for analog signal conditioning.

Chapter 5, *User Input*, presents some methods of using external hardware to interface with your BeagleBone programs, including potentiometers, buttons, and rotary encoders.

Chapter 6, *Program Output*, covers some methods of using external hardware to provide feedback to the user, from LED and LCD displays to sending e-mails and text messages.

Chapter 7, *Serial Communication*, describes in more depth the UART, I2C, and SPI serial subsystems and how they can be used to communicate with external digital devices.

Chapter 8, *Interfacing with External Devices*, walks you through the steps required to interface with a new digital device by writing a Python module to communicate with an accelerometer over I2C.

Chapter 9, *Using the Network*, shows you some ways of taking advantage of the BeagleBone Black's network connection to remotely control and monitor your applications.

Chapter 10, *A Practical Example*, walks you through using what you've learned to build a BeagleBone Black weather station with remote monitoring and automatic over/under temperature e-mail or text message alarms.

Appendix A, *The BeagleBone Black Pinout*, provides you with a visual description of the BeagleBone Black's expansion headers and the different ways each pin can be used.

Appendix B, *Disabling HDMI*, teaches you to disable the HDMI output.

What you need for this book

This book specifically targets the BeagleBone Black. It also assumes a Windows OS where setup steps are required to be run on a desktop or laptop PC, as in my experience Windows has been the main OS of folks who are just starting out with BeagleBone.

Who this book is for

If you are a Python programmer and have never had any experience with embedded Linux and hardware development, this book is for you. Some previous Linux experience will be helpful, but is not required.

Conventions

In this book, you will find a number of text styles that distinguish between different kinds of information. Here are some examples of these styles and an explanation of their meaning.

Code words in text, folder names, filenames, file extensions, pathnames, and user input are shown as follows: "This will open the `crontab` file in nano, which is a command line text editor."

A block of code is set as follows:

```
def loop():
    print "switch state:", digitalRead(SW_PIN)
    delay(250)
run(setup, loop)
```

Any command-line input or output is written as follows:

```
root@beaglebone:/var/lib/cloud9# ping -c 3 graycat.io
PING graycat.io (198.100.47.208) 56(84) bytes of data.
```

New terms and **important words** are shown in bold. Words that you see on the screen, for example, in menus or dialog boxes, appear in the text like this: "Select **Obtain IP address automatically** and click on **OK**."

 Warnings or important notes appear in a box like this.

Reader feedback

Feedback from our readers is always welcome. Let us know what you think about this book—what you liked or disliked. Reader feedback is important for us as it helps us develop titles that you will really get the most out of.

To send us general feedback, simply e-mail `feedback@packtpub.com`, and mention the book's title in the subject of your message.

If there is a topic that you have expertise in and you are interested in either writing or contributing to a book, see our author guide at `www.packtpub.com/authors`.

Customer support

Now that you are the proud owner of a Packt book, we have a number of things to help you to get the most from your purchase.

Errata

Although we have taken every care to ensure the accuracy of our content, mistakes do happen. If you find a mistake in one of our books—maybe a mistake in the text or the code—we would be grateful if you could report this to us. By doing so, you can save other readers from frustration and help us improve subsequent versions of this book. If you find any errata, please report them by visiting `http://www.packtpub.com/submit-errata`, selecting your book, clicking on the **Errata Submission Form** link, and entering the details of your errata. Once your errata are verified, your submission will be accepted and the errata will be uploaded to our website or added to any list of existing errata under the Errata section of that title.

To view the previously submitted errata, go to `https://www.packtpub.com/books/content/support` and enter the name of the book in the search field. The required information will appear under the **Errata** section.

Piracy

Piracy of copyrighted material on the Internet is an ongoing problem across all media. At Packt, we take the protection of our copyright and licenses very seriously. If you come across any illegal copies of our works in any form on the Internet, please provide us with the location address or website name immediately so that we can pursue a remedy.

Please contact us at `copyright@packtpub.com` with a link to the suspected pirated material.

We appreciate your help in protecting our authors and our ability to bring you valuable content.

Questions

If you have a problem with any aspect of this book, you can contact us at questions@packtpub.com, and we will do our best to address the problem.

Image Disclaimer

This book includes images of breadboard wiring which were generated using Fritzing (http://fritzing.org), and schematics generated using Eagle (http://cadsoftusa.com/). It also includes some screen captures of a Rigol oscilloscope.

1
Before We Begin

Before we start hooking up hardware and writing code, we'll need to have an understanding of what we're working with. This chapter will introduce you to the BeagleBone and highlight the various interfaces it provides to connect to external devices. It will cover:

- An overview of the BeagleBone system
- An overview of the BeagleBone's peripheral interfaces, and what types of external devices each can connect to
- Some additional hardware and tools that you will need if you want to duplicate the examples given throughout the book, and where you can buy them

An overview of BeagleBone

The BeagleBone boards are a series of small, powerful, and affordable Linux computers that are perfect for embedded applications such as home automation, robotics, industrial control, and much more. They are designed by BeagleBoard.org (http://beagleboard.org/) and are fully open source. They are based on the Texas Instruments AM335x 1GHz ARM Cortex-A8 series of microprocessors, and can run a number of different operating systems, including various GNU/Linux distributions, Android, and even Windows Embedded CE. The current BeagleBone model being produced is the BeagleBone Black rev C, which ships with a Debian GNU/Linux distribution. Therefore, this book will focus on using Debian on the BeagleBone Black, though much of the information given will apply to other BeagleBone models and Linux distributions as well.

The following screenshot shows the BeagleBone board:

The BeagleBone Black's AM335x microprocessor contains a number of built-in peripheral interface subsystems, enabling it to accept and generate many different forms of inputs and outputs. The BeagleBone Black includes two 2 x 23 pin rows of female header pins, giving a total of 92 connection points for hardware expansion using the processor's peripheral interface subsystems.

General purpose input/output

The **general purpose input/output** (**GPIO**) module handles all the digital input and output. In this context, *digital* refers to the fact that the signals are binary; they are either 1 or 0, represented by fully on and fully off respectively. In the case of the AM335x, the fully-on level is 3.3V, and the fully-off level is 0V. The GPIO module is used for inputs such as switches and buttons, which are either on or off. Its outputs can be used to control devices, such as LEDs, buzzers, and relays.

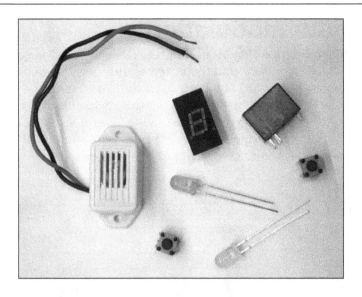

Analog-to-digital converter

The **analog-to-digital converter** (**ADC**) module is used to measure analog voltages. The AM335x ADC can only measure voltages between 0V and 1.8V (and voltages outside this range may damage your BeagleBone), but, in later chapters, you will learn how to divide larger voltages to be within this range. The ADC can be used to receive inputs from devices such as potentiometers, which can be used to create varying voltages, measure the voltage output of analog sensors for temperature, light, sound, and different types of gases, and with some additional external components it can be used to measure electrical current.

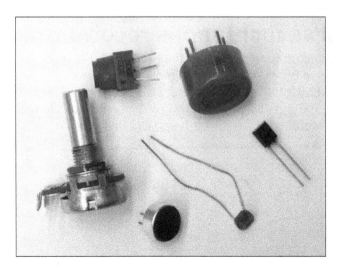

Pulse width modulation

The **pulse width modulation** (**PWM**) module is essentially used to generate a square wave signal at a fixed frequency, and then vary its duty cycle. It gives us the ability to accurately generate pulses of a configured duration, repeating at a configured frequency. Like the GPIO module, the PWM module on the BeagleBone Black operates at 3.3V. These PWM signals can be used to control servo motors, vary the speed of DC motors and the brightness of LEDs, and with some additional external components they can be used to generate varying voltages.

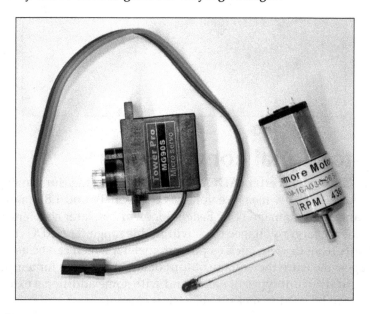

Universal asynchronous receiver/transmitter

The **universal asynchronous receiver/transmitter** (**UART**) modules are used to transmit and receive RS-232 style serial signals, which is an industry standard for serializing and transferring information between two devices using a pair of unidirectional digital signals. They can be used to communicate with PCs, Bluetooth and Wi-Fi radio modules, and GPS receivers. The BeagleBone Black's UART modules also operate at 3.3V.

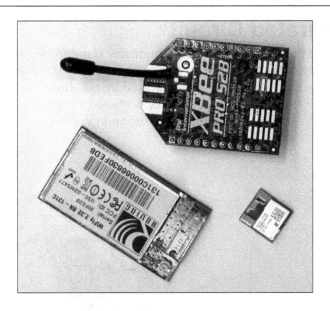

Serial peripheral interface

The **serial peripheral interface** (**SPI**) module is used to communicate over SPI, which is another industry standard serial protocol. Whereas UARTs are generally used to connect two devices, SPI is made to connect one master device to one or many slave devices. It is commonly used on devices such as small character and graphics LCD screens, external ADCs, and DACs (Digital-to-Analog converters), as well as on many different types of sensor. The BeagleBone Black's SPI modules operate at 3.3V as well.

Inter-Integrated Circuit

Inter-Integrated Circuit (I2C) is yet another industry standard serial protocol. It also allows a master device to communicate with a bus of many slave devices, but it requires fewer pins than SPI. It is commonly used by real-time clocks (RTCs), as well as in many types of sensors, including Micro-Electro-Mechanical Systems (MEMS) devices, such as accelerometers, magnetometers, and gyroscopes. The BeagleBone's I2C modules operate at 3.3V.

Tools and additional hardware

The majority of the demo programs in this book use external hardware that must be purchased separately. Each time a demo program is given, which requires additional parts, they will be listed by part number and/or description. We will do our best to use the most readily available and lowest cost parts. All of the parts used can be purchased from one or more of the following resources:

- **SparkFun**: https://www.sparkfun.com/
- **Adafruit Industries**: http://www.adafruit.com/
- **Digi-Key**: http://www.digikey.com/
- **Mouser**: http://www.mouser.com/
- **Farnell / Newark / Element14**: http://www.farnell.com/

The circuits in each demo will be assembled using solderless breadboard and jumper wires. Both come in many different shapes and sizes.

Breadboards and jumper wires can be purchased from any of the preceding links, and you'll probably want to start out with one standard-sized breadboard and a jumper wire kit, such as that from Adafruit:

- **Breadboard**: http://www.adafruit.com/products/239
- **Jumper wires**: http://www.adafruit.com/products/153

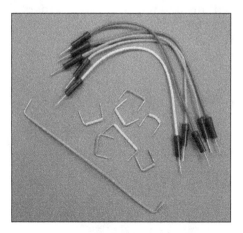

That should provide enough breadboard space and jumper wires to assemble most, if not all, of the demo circuits in this book.

Just like with software, it is inevitable when assembling hardware that things won't always work the first time. There are many tools that can greatly reduce the time it takes to fix these problems. The most useful for the circuits in this book will be a multimeter, which is a tool that measures voltage and current, and often additional properties such as resistance, capacitance, and frequency. Both SparkFun and Adafruit carry very affordable digital multimeters. While these are not high quality measurement tools, they are certainly suitable for these circuits. Though not essential, I would highly recommend having some sort of multimeter on hand when building the circuits in this book.

More helpful than a multimeter for debugging tools such as PWM and serial protocols is an oscilloscope, which shows you a plot of voltage over time to visualize many different signals in a circuit. This is a more expensive tool, and will be less necessary for these circuits. Throughout the book, however, you will see screen captures of an oscilloscope to show various signals, and it should become evident just how helpful they can be. Again, Adafruit and SparkFun carry affordable oscilloscopes.

The BeagleBone design

The BeagleBone was designed with prototyping in mind. If its shape and size look familiar to you, it's probably because the board was designed to fit inside an Altoids tin, which is great for both transportation and making custom enclosures. All of the expansion pins are broken out on to two female headers with a 2.54 mm pin pitch, which is one of the most commonly used spacings in the hobby and DIY world, and mating male header pins can easily be soldered by hand to add-on boards or wires. The board can be powered through USB or with a standard DC barrel jack, and power can also be supplied through the expansion headers.

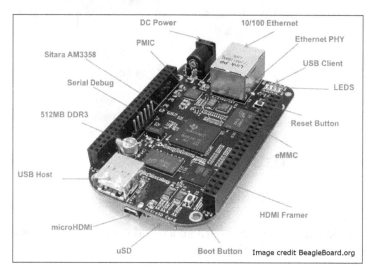

Board comparison

There are a number of low-cost single-board GNU/Linux computers on the market these days, so let's take a look at how the BeagleBone Black stacks up against a couple of its most popular competitors.

	BeagleBone Black	**Intel Edison**	**Raspberry Pi 2 B**
CPU	1 GHz single-core ARM Cortex-A8	500 MHz dual-core Intel Atom	900 MHz quad-core ARM Cortex-A7
Flash	4 GB eMMC, expandable with uSD	4 GB eMMC	uSD card
RAM	512 MB	1 GB	1 GB
Video	microHDMI	N/A	HDMI, Composite
Network	10/100 Mbit Ethernet	Dual-band a/b/g/n Wi-Fi, Bluetooth 4.0	10/100 Mbit Ethernet
GPIO pins	65	20	40
ADC channels	7	6	N/A
PWM channels	8	4	2
UARTs	4	1	1
SPI ports	2	1	1
I2C ports	2	1	2
Coprocessor	2x 200 MHz 32-bit PRU microcontrollers	100 MHz 32-bit Intel Quark	N/A
Price (USD)	$49	$49.95	$39.95

The BeagleBone Black offers great performance and far more hardware expansion capabilities at about the same cost as the Edison and Raspberry Pi 2 B. That combined with its active open source community makes it a great choice for a huge variety of projects.

Another important feature of the BeagleBone is the two built-in PRU (programmable real-time unit) microcontrollers. These are built right into the AM335x CPU and are on the ARM interconnect, so they can share memory with the ARM processor as well as provide direct access to the peripherals. This means high-speed, real-time tasks can be executed on the PRUs asynchronously without any interruption from the Linux kernel. With growing kernel driver support and documentation to compile and load firmware to PRUs, and for communicating with the code running on them from GNU/Linux user space, they really set the BeagleBone apart from much of its competition. The PRUs are outside the scope of this book, but there are plenty of tutorials and examples to be found on the Web.

Helpful resources

One of the BeagleBone Black's strong suits is the large community surrounding it.

The official site at `http://beagleboard.org/` has lots of great information.

The main source for help with BeagleBone-related issues is the mailing list at `https://groups.google.com/forum/#!forum/beagleboard`.

There are also plenty of helpful people on the #beagle IRC channel at `http://beagleboard.org/Community/Live%20Chat`.

There are also many resources online that can help fill the gaps this book leaves on the electrical side. For instance, the Element14 community at `http://www.element14.com/community/welcome` and the EEVBlog at `http://www.eevblog.com/`, both contain a wealth of great material, as well as very active electronics forums.

Summary

You should now have a better understanding of what the BeagleBone has to offer, and maybe even some insight into the types of devices we will be interfacing with in later chapters.

In the next chapter, you will be plugging in your BeagleBone Black and learning how to log in and get everything we need installed and up to date.

2
Getting Started

In this chapter, we will go through the initial steps to get your BeagleBone Black set up. By the end of it, you should be ready to write your first Python program. We will cover the following topics:

- Logging in to your BeagleBone
- Connecting to the Internet
- Updating and installing software
- The basics of the PyBBIO and Adafruit_BBIO libraries

Initial setup

If you've never turned on your BeagleBone Black, there will be a bit of initial setup required. You should follow the most up-to-date official instructions found at `http://beagleboard.org/getting-started`, but to summarize, here are the steps:

1. Install the network-over-USB drivers for your PC's operating system.
2. Plug in the USB cable between your PC and BeagleBone Black.
3. Open Chrome or Firefox and navigate to `http://192.168.7.2` (Internet Explorer is not fully supported and might not work properly).

If all goes well, you should see a message on the web page served up by the BeagleBone indicating that it has successfully connected to the USB network:

If you scroll down a little, you'll see a runnable Bonescript example, as in the following screenshot:

```
BoneScript interactive guide

BoneScript is a JavaScript library to simplify learning how to perform physical computing tasks using your
embedded Linux. This web page is able to interact with your board to provide an interactive tutorial.

Example  [ run ]  [ restore ]

  1  var b = require('bonescript');
  2  b.pinMode('USR0', b.OUTPUT);
  3  b.pinMode('USR1', b.OUTPUT);
  4  b.pinMode('USR2', b.OUTPUT);
  5  b.pinMode('USR3', b.OUTPUT);
  6  b.digitalWrite('USR0', b.HIGH);
  7  b.digitalWrite('USR1', b.HIGH);
  8  b.digitalWrite('USR2', b.HIGH);
  9  b.digitalWrite('USR3', b.HIGH);
 10  setTimeout(restore, 2000);
 11
```

If you press the **run** button you should see the four LEDs next to the Ethernet connector on your BeagleBone light up for 2 seconds and then return to their normal function of indicating system and network activity. What's happening here is the Javascript running in your browser is using the Socket.IO (http://socket.io) library to issue remote procedure calls to the Node.js server that's serving up the web page. The server then calls the Bonescript API (http://beagleboard.org/Support/BoneScript), which controls the GPIO pins connected to the LEDs. This book won't be covering Bonescript, but this example is the quickest way to control some external hardware, so it's a great place to start.

Updating your Debian image

The GNU/Linux distributions for platforms such as the BeagleBone are typically provided as ISO images, which are single file copies of the flash memory with the distribution installed. BeagleBone images are flashed onto a microSD card that the BeagleBone can then boot from. It is important to update the Debian image on your BeagleBone to ensure that it has all the most up-to-date software and drivers, which can range from important security fixes to the latest and greatest features. First, grab the latest BeagleBone Black Debian image from http://beagleboard.org/latest-images. You should now have a .img.xz file, which is an ISO image with XZ compression.

Before the image can be flashed from a Windows PC, you'll have to decompress it. Install 7-Zip (`http://www.7-zip.org/`), which will let you decompress the file from the context menu by right-clicking on it.

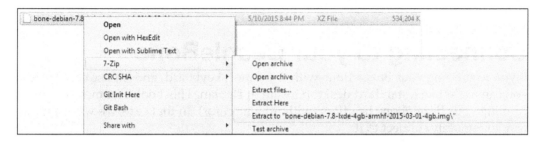

You can install Win32 Disk Imager (`http://sourceforge.net/projects/win32diskimager/`) to flash the decompressed `.img` file to your microSD card. Plug the microSD card you want your BeagleBone Black to boot from into your PC and launch Win32 Disk Imager. Select the drive letter associated with your microSD card; this process will erase the target device, so make sure the correct device is selected:

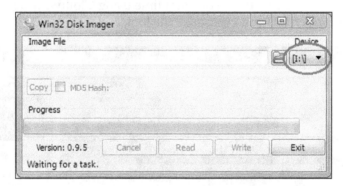

Next, press the browse button and select the decompressed `.img` file, then press **Write**:

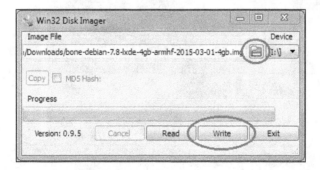

The image burning process will take a few minutes. Once it is complete, you can eject the microSD card, insert it into the BeagleBone Black and boot it up. You can then return to `http://192.168.7.2` to make sure the new image was flashed successfully and the BeagleBone is able to boot.

Connecting to your BeagleBone

If you're running your BeagleBone with a monitor, keyboard, and mouse connected, you can use it like a standard desktop install of Debian. This book assumes you are running your BeagleBone headless (without a monitor). In that case, we will need a way to remotely connect to it.

The Cloud9 IDE

The BeagleBone Debian images include an instance of the Cloud9 IDE (`https://c9.io`) running on port 3000. To access it, simply navigate to your BeagleBone Black's IP address with the port appended after a colon, that is, `http://192.168.7.2:3000`. If it's your first time using Cloud9, you'll see the welcome screen, which lets you customize the look and feel:

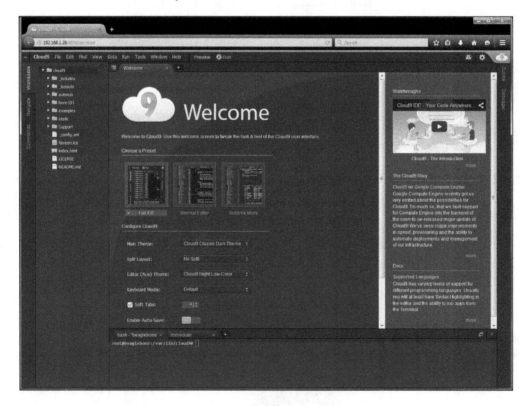

The left panel lets you organize, create, and delete files in your Cloud9 workspace. When you open a file for editing, it is shown in the center panel, and the lower panel holds a Bash shell and a Javascript REPL. Files and terminal instances can be opened in both the center and bottom panels. Bash instances start in the Cloud9 workspace, but you can use them to navigate anywhere on the BeagleBone's filesystem. If you've never used the Bash shell I'd encourage you to take a look at the Bash manual (`https://www.gnu.org/software/bash/manual/`), as well as walk through a tutorial or two. It can be very helpful and even essential at times, to be able to use Bash, especially with a platform such as BeagleBone without a monitor connected.

Another great use for the Bash terminal in Cloud9 is for running the Python interactive interpreter, which you can launch in the terminal by running `python` without any arguments:

```
python - "beaglebone ×    +

root@beaglebone:/var/lib/cloud9# python
Python 2.7.3 (default, Mar 14 2014, 17:55:54)
[GCC 4.6.3] on linux2
Type "help", "copyright", "credits" or "license" for more information.
>>> print "Hello, world!"
Hello, world!
>>>
```

SSH

If you're a Linux user, or if you would prefer not to be doing your development through a web browser, you may want to use SSH to access your BeagleBone instead. SSH, or Secure Shell, is a protocol for securely gaining terminal access to a remote computer over a network. On Windows, you can download PuTTY from `http://www.chiark.greenend.org.uk/~sgtatham/putty/download.html`, which can act as an SSH client.

Run PuTTY, make sure SSH is selected, and enter your BeagleBone's IP address and the default SSH port of 22:

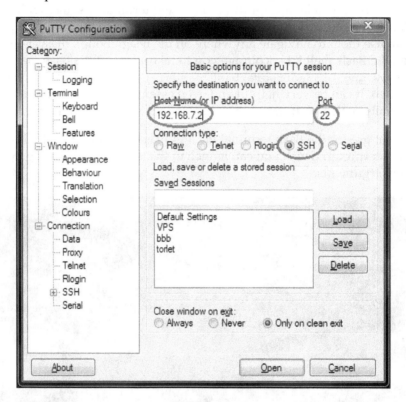

When you press **Open**, PuTTY will open an SSH connection to your BeagleBone and give you a terminal window (the first time you connect to your BeagleBone it will ask you if you trust the SSH key; press **Yes**). Enter `root` as the username and press *Enter* to log in; you will be dropped into a Bash terminal:

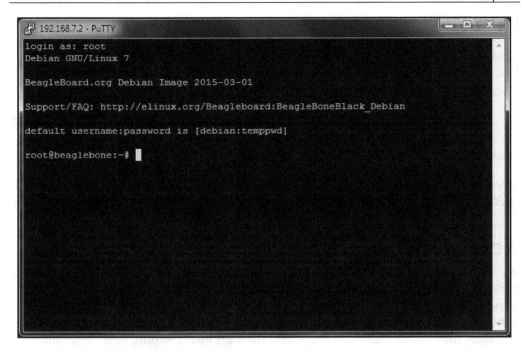

As in the Cloud9 IDE's terminals, from here, you can use the Linux tools to move around the filesystem, create and edit files, and so on, and you can run the Python interactive interpreter to try out and debug Python code.

Connecting to the Internet

Your BeagleBone Black won't be able to access the Internet with the default network-over-USB configuration, but there are a couple ways that you can connect your BeagleBone to the Internet.

Ethernet

The simplest option is to connect the BeagleBone to your network using an Ethernet cable between your BeagleBone and your router or a network switch. When the BeagleBone Black boots with an Ethernet connection, it will use DHCP to automatically request an IP address and register on your network.

Once you have your BeagleBone registered on your network, you'll be able to log in to your router's interface from your web browser (usually found at `http://192.168.1.1` or `http://192.168.2.1`) and find out the IP address that was assigned to your BeagleBone. Refer to your router's manual for more information. The current BeagleBone Black Debian images are configured to use the hostname `beaglebone`, so it should be pretty easy to find in your router's client list. If you are using a network on which you have no way of accessing this information through the router, you could use a tool such as Fing (`http://www.overlooksoft.com`) for Android or iPhone to scan the network and list the IP addresses of every device on it.

Since this method results in your BeagleBone being assigned a new IP address, you'll need to use the new address to access the Getting Started pages and the Cloud9 IDE.

Network forwarding

If you don't have access to an Ethernet connection, or it's just more convenient to have your BeagleBone connected to your computer instead of your router, it is possible to forward your Internet connection to your BeagleBone over the USB network. On Windows, open your **Network Connections** window by navigating to it from the Control Panel or by opening the start menu, typing `ncpa.cpl`, and pressing *Enter*. Locate the **Linux USB Ethernet** network interface and take note of the name; in my case, its **Local Area Network 4**. This is the network interface used to connect to your BeagleBone:

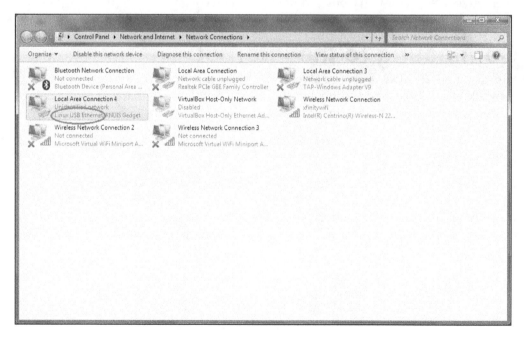

First, right-click on the network interface that you are accessing the Internet through, in my case, **Wireless Network Connection**, and select **Properties**. On the **Sharing** tab, check **Allow other network users to connect through this computer's Internet connection**, and select your BeagleBone's network interface from the dropdown:

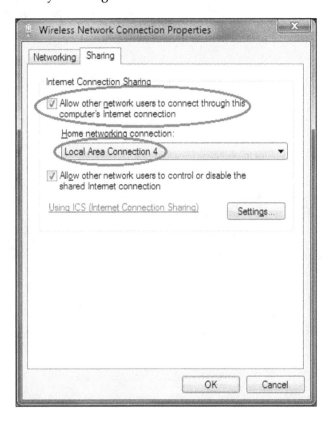

After pressing **OK**, Windows will assign the BeagleBone interface a static IP address, which will conflict with the static IP address of http://192.168.7.2 that the BeagleBone is configured to request on the USB network interface. To fix this, you'll want to right-click the **Linux USB Ethernet** interface and select **Properties**, then highlight **Internet Protocol Version 4 (TCP/IPv4)** and click on **Properties**:

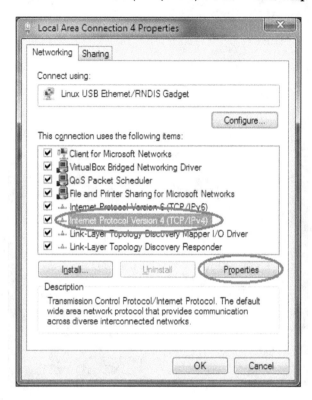

Select **Obtain IP address automatically** and click on **OK**;

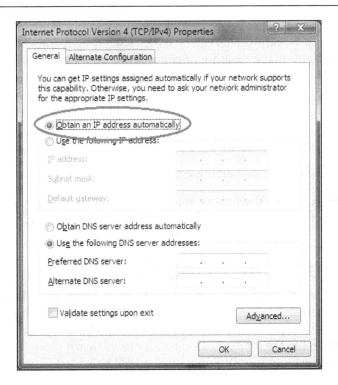

Your Windows PC is now forwarding its Internet connection to the BeagleBone, but the BeagleBone is still not configured properly to access the Internet. The problem is that the BeagleBone's IP routing table doesn't include 192.168.7.1 as a gateway, so it doesn't know the network path to the Internet. Access a Cloud9 or SSH terminal, and use the route tool to add the gateway, as shown in the following command:

```
# route add default gw 192.168.7.1
```

Your BeagleBone should now have Internet access, which you can test by pinging a website:

```
root@beaglebone:/var/lib/cloud9# ping -c 3 graycat.io
PING graycat.io (198.100.47.208) 56(84) bytes of data.
64 bytes from 198.100.47.208.static.a2webhosting.com (198.100.47.208):
icmp_req=1 ttl=55 time=45.6 ms
64 bytes from 198.100.47.208.static.a2webhosting.com (198.100.47.208):
icmp_req=2 ttl=55 time=45.6 ms
64 bytes from 198.100.47.208.static.a2webhosting.com (198.100.47.208):
icmp_req=3 ttl=55 time=46.0 ms

--- graycat.io ping statistics ---
3 packets transmitted, 3 received, 0% packet loss, time 2002ms
rtt min/avg/max/mdev = 45.641/45.785/46.035/0.248 ms
```

The IP routing will be reset at boot up, so if you reboot your BeagleBone, the Internet connection will stop working. This can be easily solved by using Cron, a Linux tool for scheduling the automatic running of commands. To add the correct gateway at boot, you'll need to edit the `crontab` file with the following command:

```
# crontab -e
```

This will open the `crontab` file in nano, which is a command line text editor. We can use the `@reboot` keyword to schedule the command to run after each reboot:

```
@reboot /sbin/route add default gw 192.168.7.1
```

Press *Ctrl* + *X* to exit nano, then press *Y*, and then *Enter* to save the file. Your forwarded Internet connection should now remain after rebooting.

Using the serial console

If you are unable to use a network connection to your BeagleBone Black; for instance, if your network is too slow for Cloud9 or you can't find the BeagleBone's IP address, there is still hope! The BeagleBone Black includes a 6-pin male connector; labeled J1, right next to the P9 expansion header (we'll learn more about the P8 and P9 expansion headers soon!). You'll need a USB to 3.3 V TTL serial converter, for example, from Adafruit http://www.adafruit.com/products/70 or Logic Supply http://www.logicsupply.com/components/beaglebone/accessories/ls-ttl3vt. You'll need to download and install the FTDI virtual COM port driver for your operating system from http://www.ftdichip.com/Drivers/VCP.htm, then plug the connector into the J1 header such that the black wire lines up with the header's pin 1 indicator, as shown in the following screenshot:

You can then use your favorite serial port terminal emulator, such as PuTTY or CoolTerm (`http://freeware.the-meiers.org`), and configure the serial port for a baud rate of 115200 with 1 stop bit and no parity. Once connected, press *Enter* and you should see a login prompt. Enter the user name `root` and you'll drop into a Bash shell. If you only need the console connection to find your IP address, you can do so using the following command:

```
# ip addr
```

Updating your software

If this is the first time you've booted your BeagleBone Black, or if you've just flashed a new image, it's best to start by ensuring your installed software packages are all up to date. You can do so using Debian's `apt` package manager:

```
# apt-get update && apt-get upgrade
```

This process might take a few minutes.

Next, use the `pip` Python package manager to update to the latest versions of the `PyBBIO` and `Adafruit_BBIO` libraries:

```
# pip install --upgrade PyBBIO Adafruit_BBIO
```

As both libraries are currently in active development, it's worth running this command from time to time to make sure you have all the latest features.

The PyBBIO library

The `PyBBIO` library was developed with Arduino users in mind. It emulates the structure of an Arduino (`http://arduino.cc`) program, as well as the Arduino API where appropriate. If you've never seen an Arduino program, it consists of a `setup()` function, which is called once when the program starts, and a `loop()` function, which is called repeatedly until the end of time (or until you turn off the Arduino). `PyBBIO` accomplishes a similar structure by defining a `run()` function that is passed two callable objects, one that is called once when the program starts, and another that is called repeatedly until the program stops. So the basic `PyBBIO` template looks like this:

```
from bbio import *

def setup():
```

```
  pinMode(GPIO1_16, OUTPUT)

def loop():
  digitalWrite(GPIO1_16, HIGH)
  delay(500)
  digitalWrite(GPIO1_16, LOW)
  delay(500)

run(setup, loop)
```

The first line imports everything from the PyBBIO library (the Python package is installed with the name bbio). Then, two functions are defined, and they are passed to run(), which tells the PyBBIO loop to begin. In this example, setup() will be called once, which configures the GPIO pin GPIO1_16 as a digital output with the pinMode() function. Then, loop() will be called until the PyBBIO loop is stopped, with each digitalWrite() call setting the GPIO1_16 pin to either a high (on) or low (off) state, and each delay() call causing the program to sleep for 500 milliseconds. The loop can be stopped by either pressing *Ctrl + C* or calling the stop() function. Any other error raised in your program will be caught, allowing PyBBIO to run any necessary cleanup, then it will be reraised. Don't worry if the program doesn't make sense yet, we'll learn about all that soon!

Not everyone wants to use the Arduino style loop, and it's not always suitable depending on the program you're writing. PyBBIO can also be used in a more Pythonic way, for example, the above program can be rewritten as follows:

```
import bbio

bbio.pinMode(bbio.GPIO1_16, bbio.OUTPUT)
while True:
  bbio.digitalWrite(bbio.GPIO1_16, bbio.HIGH)
  bbio.delay(500)
  bbio.digitalWrite(bbio.GPIO1_16, bbio.LOW)
  bbio.delay(500)
```

This still allows the bbio API to be used, but it is kept out of the global namespace.

The Adafruit_BBIO library

The Adafruit_BBIO library is structured differently than PyBBIO. While PyBBIO is structured such that, essentially, the entire API is accessed directly from the first level of the bbio package; Adafruit_BBIO instead has the package tree broken up by a peripheral subsystem. For instance, to use the GPIO API you have to import the GPIO package:

```
from Adafruit_BBIO import GPIO
```

Otherwise, to use the PWM API you would import the PWM package:

```
from Adafruit_BBIO import PWM
```

This structure follows a more standard Python library model, and can also save some space in your program's memory because you're only importing the parts you need (the difference is pretty minimal, but it is worth thinking about).

The same program shown above using PyBBIO could be rewritten to use Adafruit_BBIO:

```
from Adafruit_BBIO import GPIO
import time

GPIO.setup("GPIO1_16", GPIO.OUT)
try:
  while True:
    GPIO.output("GPIO1_16", GPIO.HIGH)
    time.sleep(0.5)
    GPIO.output("GPIO1_16", GPIO.LOW)
    time.sleep(0.5)
except KeyboardInterrupt:
  GPIO.cleanup()
```

Here the GPIO.setup() function is configuring the ping, and GPIO.output() is setting the state. Notice that we needed to import Python's built-in time library to sleep, whereas in PyBBIO we used the built-in delay() function. We also needed to explicitly catch KeyboardInterrupt (the *Ctrl + C* signal) to make sure all the cleanup is run before the program exits, whereas this is done automatically by PyBBIO. Of course, this means that you have much more control about when things such as initialization and cleanup happen using Adafruit_BBIO, which can be very beneficial depending on your program. There are some trade-offs, and the library you use should be chosen based on which model is better suited for your application.

Summary

In this chapter, you learned how to login to the BeagleBone Black, get it connected to the Internet, and update and install the software we need. We also looked at the basic structure of programs using the `PyBBIO` and `Adafruit_BBIO` libraries, and talked about some of the advantages of each.

In the next chapter, you will learn how to use the GPIO pins to control some LEDs!

3
Digital Outputs

In this chapter, you will learn the basics of GPIO outputs and driving LEDs, as well as some of the features of the Cloud9 IDE. We will cover the following topics:

- How GPIO pins are configured
- Using the Python interactive prompt to control digital outputs
- Calculating current limiting resistor values for LEDs
- Using NPN transistors to drive LEDs from GPIO pins
- Blinking an LED continuously with a Python program
- Running multiple programs at once to blink multiple LEDs
- Running programs on startup

GPIO modules

The BeagleBone Black has up to 69 different GPIO pins available on its expansion headers. These GPIO signals are controlled through four separate 32-signal GPIO modules, named GPIO0, GPIO1, GPIO2, and GPIO3. Each pin can either be put into output mode, where it can then be set to a 3.3 V high level or a 0 V low level, or input mode, where it can sense whether the level on the pin is high or low.

Kernel drivers

The GPIO modules inside microprocessors are typically controlled by reading and writing their memory registers directly. Like many other single board Linux computers, the BeagleBone provides a kernel driver which interacts with the GPIO memory registers for you, and is controlled via a `sysfs` interface.

`Sysfs` is a virtual file system in the Linux kernel, consisting of special virtual files that provide input to and output from kernel drivers for configuring and controlling buses and devices.

The `sysfs` entries for the BeagleBone Black's GPIO driver reside in `/sys/class/gpio/`. Both PyBBIO and Adafruit_BBIO use these sysfs entries for GPIO access.

Pin multiplexing

The physical pins on the BeagleBone's microprocessor are not connected directly to the GPIO modules. Instead, they are connected to the outputs of internal multiplexers, which allow the functionality of each physical pin to be selected programmatically. This allows all of the possible I/O signals to be used, which is far more than the number of physical pins. It also means that there is an additional step required to select the function of each pin before they can be used.

The pin multiplexing, or pinmuxing, cannot be done from user space on the BeagleBone Black. Instead, it is done through the Device Tree, which is a data structure in the Linux kernel that describes the hardware of the machine it is running on. The state of the pin multiplexers can be set through Device Tree overlays, which are sections of the Device Tree structure that can be applied on top of the base Device Tree description to change its default configurations. This can either be done at boot time or, on the BeagleBone Black, through the `capemgr` kernel driver at run time.

PyBBIO has its own Device Tree overlays that it dynamically loads using `capemgr`, so pinmuxing is done automatically when using PyBBIO. Adafruit_BBIO doesn't handle pinmuxing, so when using it, you'll have to do it manually. Luckily, this is made easy through Charles Steinkuehler's universal-io Device Tree overlay and config-pin command line tool (`https://github.com/cdsteinkuehler/beaglebone-universal-io`), which, together, let you configure any of the processor's pin multiplexers. You can load the universal-io overlay at runtime from a terminal on your BeagleBone Black (through SSH or Cloud9) using the `capemgr` kernel driver. The command is as follows:

```
# echo cape-universaln > /sys/devices/bone_capemgr.*/slots
```

Writing this to the `slots` file tells `capemgr` to apply the Device Tree overlay called `cape-universaln`, which comes compiled with the BeagleBone's kernel. There are a few different versions of the universal-io overlay; most of the pins on the P8 header are in use by the HDMI interface, and this version with an 'n' at the end does not include those pins. HDMI is enabled by default, and si006Ece `capemgr` won't allow you to load an overlay that includes pins that are already in use, this is the only version that will work without disabling HDMI, which is explained in *Appendix A, The BeagleBone Black Pinout*.

Since `capemgr` won't load overlays with conflicting pins, the universal-io overlay is incompatible with PyBBIO's custom overlays. This means that PyBBIO and Adafruit_BBIO programs shouldn't be run at the same time, so if you're running multiple Python programs asynchronously, you'll want to stick to just one library. A reboot is required to reset the loaded overlays.

Interactive GPIO

Let's take a look at how the GPIO pins can be controlled from Python's interactive interpreter. Enter the Python interpreter by running the `python` command without any arguments into a terminal (either in Cloud9 or in an SSH session), as shown in the following command:

```
root@beaglebone:/var/lib/cloud9# python
Python 2.7.3 (default, Mar 14 2014, 17:55:54)
[GCC 4.6.3] on linux2
Type "help", "copyright", "credits" or "license" for more information.
>>>
```

Next, import everything from the PyBBIO library:

```
>>> from bbio import *
```

Now let's light one of the BeagleBone's on-board LEDs. Use the `digitalWrite()` function to set the GPIO output attached to the USR3 LED to its high level:

```
>>> digitalWrite(USR3, HIGH)
```

Take a look at **USER LEDS** closest to the Ethernet connector on your BeagleBone, it should now be lit up, as shown in the following screenshot:

Go ahead and turn it off by setting it to a low state:

```
>>> digitalWrite(USR3, LOW)
```

Congratulations, you've just blinked your first LED from your BeagleBone Black. It's not really that satisfying to just blink the on-board LEDs though, so let's hook up an external one.

For this circuit, you will need:

- Breadboard
- 1x 5 mm LED
- 1x 330 Ω resistor
- Jumper wires

Hook the components up on your breadboard, as shown in the following screenshot:

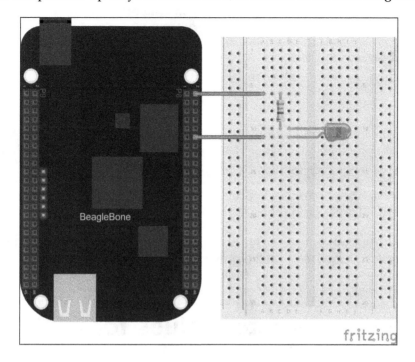

LEDs only work when current flows into their anode (longer pin) and out of their cathode (shorter pin), so be sure to hook it up the right way. The LED is shown in the following screenshot:

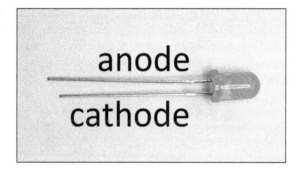

With the LED and resistor hooked up to P8.12, we can return to the interactive prompt to try it out, this time using `GPIO1_12` instead of `USR3`:

```
>>> from bbio import *
>>> pinMode(GPIO1_12, OUTPUT)
>>> digitalWrite(GPIO1_12, HIGH)
```

Note that we called `pinMode()` this time, which does three things:

- Sets the internal pin multiplexer to connect the `GPIO1_12` signal to the P8.12 header pin (using the custom Device Tree overlays described previously)
- Sets pin 12 of the GPIO1 module as an output
- Reserves the pin for user space control, meaning the kernel won't change its state until it has been returned to kernel space control

We didn't have to call `pinMode()` for the USR3 LED earlier because the Linux kernel on the BeagleBone sets up those pins at boot, but it is required for all other GPIO pins.

Calculating resistor values for LEDs

Let's take a moment to talk about driving LEDs. There's plenty of information out there on how LEDs operate, and to be honest, we don't need to think about the majority of it. That's not to say that it's not a fascinating subject, but there's really only two properties we care about here—the forward voltage and the forward current. The forward voltage, also called the forward voltage drop or just voltage drop, of an LED is the voltage that is dropped across it, and the forward current is the maximum current that the LED can handle without being damaged. Both these values vary between different LEDs, but general purpose 3 mm and 5 mm LEDs like the one pictured previously will typically have a forward voltage of around 2 V and a forward current of around 20 mA.

The simplest way to limit the current through the LED to the desired forward current is by using a resistor in series with it. Let's take a look at the following diagram:

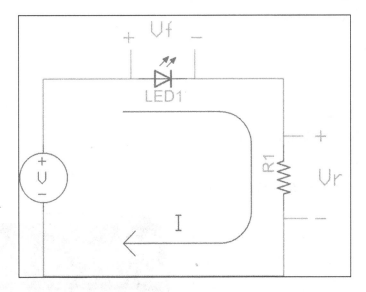

Let's assume the voltage source in this diagram (**V**) is 3.3 V. If the LED has a **forward voltage (Vf)** of 2 V, then that means the voltage across the resistor, labeled **Vr**, is *3.3 V - 2 V = 1.3 V*. Ohm's law tells us that the voltage across a resistor in volts is equivalent to the product of the current through it in amps and its resistance in ohms, that is, *V = IR*. If we want a forward current through the LED (**I**) of 20 mA, we can use Ohm's law to calculate the proper resistor value, *R = 1.3 V / 0.02 A = 65 Ω*. Resistors only come in certain values, so we want to round that up to the nearest standard value of 68 Ω.

 Resistor values are measured in ohms, named after Georg Simon Ohm, a German physicist who discovered the relationship between voltage and current, which is the basis of what we now call Ohm's law. Ohms are notated by the capital Greek omega (Ω).

Driving higher currents from GPIO pins

We just calculated that a 68 Ω resistor will give us the maximum forward current from a 3.3 V supply, but when we hooked up the LED to the 3.3 V GPIO pin earlier, we used a 330 Ω resistor. This is because the GPIO pins of BeagleBone's processor are only rated to source a maximum current of 4-6 mA. Using a 330 Ω resistor gives *1.3 V / 330 Ω = 3.9 mA*.

There are a few ways we can source more current than the 4-6 mA maximum of the GPIO pins; one simple way is to use an NPN **Bipolar Junction Transistor (BJT)**.

For this circuit, you will need:

- Breadboard
- 1x 5 mm LED
- 1x 4.7 kΩ resistor
- 1x 68 Ω resistor
- 1x 2N3904 NPN transistor
- Jumper wires

Wire it up on your breadboard as shown here:

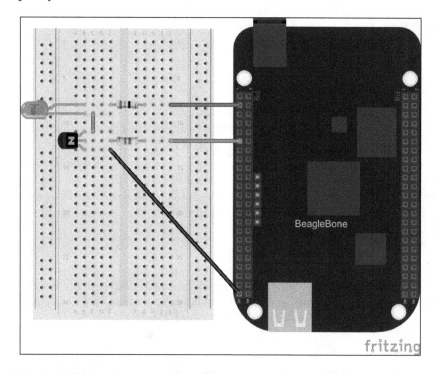

 If you have a resistor kit like the one from SparkFun (`https://www.sparkfun.com/products/10969`) you might not have a 68 Ω resistor handy. If this is the case, you can use one 220 Ω resistor in parallel with one 100 Ω resistor for a combined resistance of 68.75 Ω.

Let's take a quick look at a schematic for this circuit:

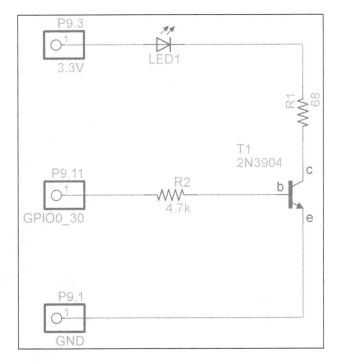

There is tons to be learned about transistors, but in this case, we're essentially using it as a switch, and we can treat it as a black box. When the GPIO pin is set to its 0 V low state, no current flows into the base of the transistor (marked **b** in the schematic), which prevents any current from flowing between the collector (**c**) and the emitter (**e**). When the GPIO pin is set high, enough current flows through **R2** into the base of the transistor to allow it to pass a larger current (by a current gain factor, which is a specified parameter of the specific transistor being used) from the collector (**c**) to the emitter (**e**), and therefore, through the **LED1** and **R1**. This basically allows you to switch on and off the current flowing through the LED directly from the 3.3 V power supply, and the 68 Ω resistor limits it to the 20 mA we need.

If you put an ammeter in series with the LED and measure the current through it, you will see that it is actually a bit lower than 20 mA. This is because there is a slight voltage across the transistor's collector and emitter. This voltage drop is proportional to the current, so it can be tricky to calculate the exact resistor value needed, but with an ammeter and a bit of trial and error, you can narrow it down to a good value. A 56 Ω resistor should give around 19.5 mA with the 2N3904.

Blink

Now that we have our transistor driving the LED at its full current from GPIO0_30 (P9.11), let's use Adafruit_BBIO to write a program that blinks it at a fixed interval. The first step is to load the universal-io Device Tree overlay as described previously:

```
# echo cape-universaln > /sys/devices/bone_capemgr.*/slots
```

Next you'll need to use the `config-pin` command to manually configure the pin as a digital output:

```
# config-pin P9_11 in
```

Now that the pin is configured properly, open a new file in Cloud9 called `blink.py` with the following code:

```python
from Adafruit_BBIO import GPIO
import time

LED_PIN = "GPIO0_30"
GPIO.setup(LED_PIN, GPIO.OUT)

while True:
  GPIO.output(LED_PIN, GPIO.HIGH)
  time.sleep(0.5)
  GPIO.output(LED_PIN, GPIO.LOW)
  time.sleep(0.5)
```

Press **Run** and you should see the LED turn on for half a second, turn off for half a second, and repeat forever. Alright! When you're done watching the light show you can press the **Stop** button or hit *Ctrl + C* in the terminal that opened when the program started to kill it.

Taking advantage of the OS

Since the BeagleBone is running a full GNU/Linux operating system, there are plenty of great tools available for us to take advantage of. Let's look at a couple of the advantages an OS gives you.

Multiprocessing

Every time you click on **Run** in Cloud9, it launches the program as a new process, so you can easily run many different programs simultaneously. Let's add a second transistor/LED circuit, this time using GPIO3_19 on P9.27.

For this, you will need:

- Breadboard
- 2x 5 mm LED
- 2x 4.7 kΩ resistor
- 2x 68 Ω resistor
- 2x 2N3904 NPN transistor
- Jumper wires

Wire it up on your breadboard as shown here:

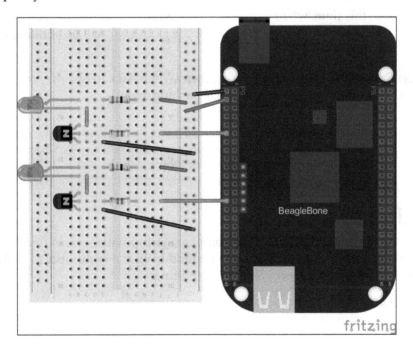

Now create a new file called `blink2.py`, and this time, let's use `PyBBIO`, as shown in the following code:

```
from bbio import *

LED_PIN = GPIO3_19

def setup():
  pinMode(LED_PIN, OUTPUT)

def loop():
  digitalWrite(LED_PIN, HIGH)
  delay(250)
  digitalWrite(LED_PIN, LOW)
  delay(250)

run(setup, loop)
```

As you can see, this time, we're delaying the loop by 250 milliseconds or a quarter of a second, each time we change the state of the LED, so it will be blinking twice as fast.

Now press **Run** with `blink2.py` in focus, then switch back to `blink1.py` and press **Run** again. You should now see both LEDs flashing away.

 Note that each time you press **Run** it will open a new terminal tab in the bottom pane. To kill a specific program, you'll have to select its corresponding tab before pressing **Stop**.

Running at startup

We've already looked at running a command at startup with `Cron` in *Chapter 2, Getting Started*, and we can use this same method to start any number of Python programs at boot. Open the `crontab` file for editing:

```
# crontab -e
```

Now add a new line to launch your program:

```
@reboot /usr/bin/python /path/to/my_program.py
```

We need to use the full path to the Python executable because the commands in the `crontab` file are run with a minimal set of environment variables, which doesn't include the PATH variable that usually tells your terminal where to search for executables. You'll also need the full path to your Python script. If it's saved inside the Cloud9 workspace, then it will start with `/var/lib/cloud9/`.

Summary

In this chapter, you learned how to use the GPIO pins as outputs to drive LEDs (GPIO inputs will be covered in *Chapter 5*, *User Input*, so stay tuned!). We used both the on-board LEDs, as well as external LEDs that we wired up ourselves. You learned about the current sourcing limitations of the BeagleBone's GPIO pins, as well as how to use an NPN transistor to source higher currents from them. You learned how to use Cloud9 to run Python programs that drive the LEDs, and how to run multiple programs simultaneously and automatically at startup.

In the next chapter, you will learn about pulse width modulation and the analog-to-digital converters.

4
PWM and ADC Subsystems

In this chapter, we will take a look at the **pulse width modulation** (**PWM**) and **analog-to-digital converter** (**ADC**) subsystems. We will cover the following topics:

- Fading an LED
- Controlling servo motors
- Voltage dividers
- Voltage followers
- Sensing light levels with a photocell
- Sensing distance with Sharp IR rangefinders
- Building a simple robot

PWM

The BeagleBone's PWM subsystem contains three enhanced PWM (ePWM) modules and one enhanced capture (eCAP) module, all of which have their own two outputs, for a total of up to eight PWM outputs (refer to *Appendix A*, *The BeagleBone Black Pinout* to see which pins support PWM). We briefly covered what PWM is in *Chapter 1*, *Before We Begin*, but let's look at it in a bit more detail before we start using it.

For this, you will need:

- Breadboard
- 1x 5 mm LED
- 1x 4.7 kΩ resistor
- 1x 68 Ω resistor
- 1x 2N3904 NPN transistor
- Jumper wires

Let's start by wiring up an LED with an NPN transistor as we did in *Chapter 3, Digital Outputs*; only this time, we will drive it with the ePWM1 module's 'A' output on P9.14:

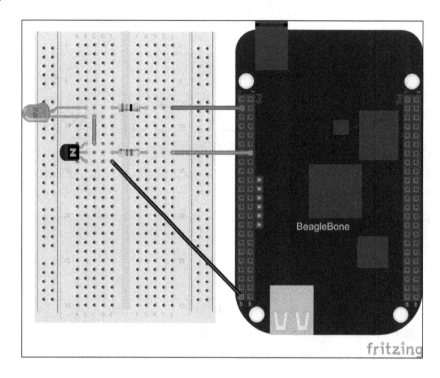

Now let's fire up the Python interactive interpreter and configure the PWM output at 50 percent duty cycle:

```
>>> from bbio import *
>>> analogWrite(PWM1A, 50, 100)
```

You should see the LED turn on, but dimmer than if you had driven it with a GPIO pin. So what's going on here? The analogWrite() function is used to set the duty cycle of the output signal, and in this case, we've told it to drive the output high for 50/100 or 50 percent of the cycle. This percentage is called the **duty cycle**. Let's take a look at the signal now being generated on the PWM1A pin with an oscilloscope:

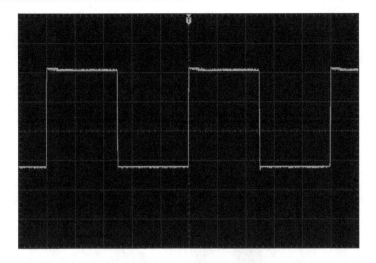

You might be wondering why you can't see the LED blinking on and off; the actual frequency of the output defaults to 10 KHz in PyBBIO, or 2 KHz in Adafruit_BBIO, meaning there are 10,000 or 2,000 of these half-on half-off cycles every second respectively. Those changes are much faster than the human eye can perceive, so we just see it as being dimmer.

Now let's set the output down to 10 percent:

```
>>> analogWrite(PWM1A, 10, 100)
```

And here's what a 10 percent duty cycle looks like on the oscilloscope:

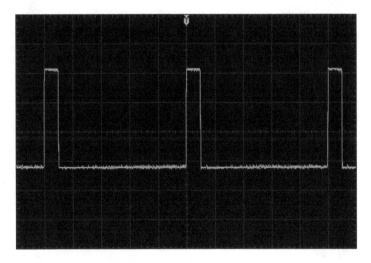

With the LED only lit for 10 percent of the cycle, we perceive it as being dimly lit. Now if we go up to a 90 percent duty cycle, the LED looks much brighter:

```
>>> analogWrite(PWM1A, 90, 100)
```

And, as expected, we can see on the oscilloscope that the signal is high for 90 percent of its period:

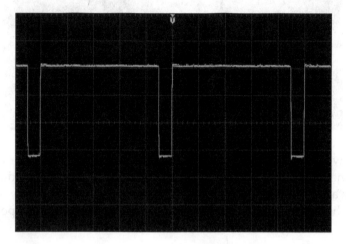

The first time the `analogWrire()` function is called it automatically enables the the PWM subsystem and configures the pin multiplexer for PWM output by loading Device Tree overlays using the `capemgr` driver.

Fading an LED

Try out this example program with the same transistor-LED circuit as before, which will fade the LED up and down forever:

```python
from bbio import *
led_pin = PWM1A
def setup():
  pass
  def loop():
    for level in range(0, 255, 5):
      analogWrite(led_pin, level)
      delay(10)
    for level in range(255, 0, -5):
      analogWrite(led_pin, level)
      delay(10)
run(setup, loop)
```

As you can see, we're going all the way up to a PWM value of 255 this time, and we've left out the third argument to the `analogWrite()` function. That third argument is optional, and defines the resolution being used. It defaults to 256 to be consistent with the Arduino `analogWrite()` routine, but it can be any number, for instance, 100 to specify values in percent. The BeagleBone's PWM modules use 16-bit timers, so the actual maximum resolution is 216 or 65536.

Now let's take a look at how PWM is used in `Adafruit_BBIO`:

```
import time
from Adafruit_BBIO import PWM

led_pin = "P9_14"
PWM.start(led_pin, 0)

try:
  while True:
    for level in range(0, 100):
      PWM.set_duty_cycle(led_pin, level)
      time.sleep(0.01)
    for level in range(100, 0, -1):
      PWM.set_duty_cycle(led_pin, level)
      time.sleep(0.01)
except KeyboardInterrupt:
  PWM.cleanup()
```

The second argument passed `PWM.start()` is the initial duty cycle. `Adafruit_BBIO` also lets you change the PWM frequency, which it sets to 2 kHz by default, by passing the desired frequency in Hz as a third argument to `PWM.start()`. The `Adafruit_BBIO` PWM outputs are set by their duty cycle in percent, so `PWM.set_duty_cycle()` takes values in the range 0–100, which can float point numbers for higher resolutions. Like with PyBBIO, the first time `PWM.start()` is called the appropriate Device Tree overlays will be loaded.

Servo motors

A common device that is controlled by PWM is the servo motor. Standard micro servos, such as the Tower Pro SG92R, are readily available at stores such as SparkFun and Adafruit, and are a cheap and easy way to get things moving. Let's take a look at controlling a micro servo from the BeagleBone.

For this, you will need:

- Breadboard
- 1x 1 kΩ resistor
- 1x 0.1 µF capacitor
- 1x micro servo motor
- Jumper wires

Wire the servo to the BeagleBone's 5 V supply, and connect the signal wire to PWM1A through a 1 kΩ resistor:

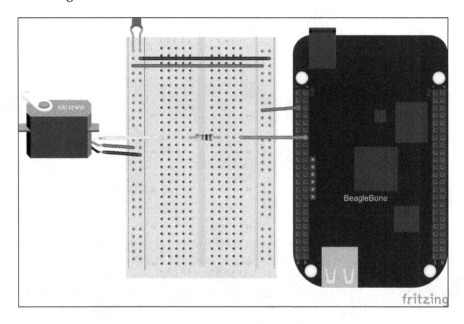

The BeagleBone P9 header has two different 5 V supplies. P9.5 and P9.6 are connected directly to the DC barrel jack, and P9.7 and P9.8 are connected to the output of the BeagleBone's on-board voltage regulator. If you are powering your BeagleBone from the DC barrel jack, it is best to use P9.5 and P9.6 as you will be able to draw more current. If you are powering the BeagleBone through the USB jack you will have to use P9.7 and P9.8 instead, in which case your connected devices cannot draw more than 250 mA.

The 1 kΩ resistor ensures that the servo can't draw too much current from the PWM pin.

The 0.1 μF (0.1 microfarad) capacitor across the power supply is being used as what's called a bypass capacitor. One of the properties of capacitors is that they pass high frequency signals and block low-frequency and DC signals. A bypass capacitor essentially shorts any high frequency signals that may be coupled on the power supply to ground, leaving a clean DC supply. It is not necessarily required as the BeagleBone has its own bypass capacitors on board, but it is advised as we are adding a servo motor, which can draw quick pulses of current and couple high frequency signals onto the supply.

A servo motor can typically only rotate 180 degrees at most, and it will position itself at a given angle depending on the width of the positive pulse of the input signal. Typically, they require an input signal of around 50 Hz, with a positive pulse of around 0.5 ms for 0 degrees and up to around 2.4 ms for 180 degrees. With the motor connected, let's launch the Python interpreter and give it a go.

First, let's set the frequency of the ePWM1 module to 50 Hz:

```
>>> from bbio import *
>>> pwmFrequency(PWM1A, 50)
```

We could figure out the duty cycles as percentages for the desired pulse widths, or to make it easier, we can just use the period of a full cycle as our resolution *period = 1 / 50*, *Hz = 0.02*, and *s = 20 ms*. So to set the positive pulse to 0.5 ms, we can use the following command line:

```
>>> analogWrite(PWM1A, 0.5, 20)
```

To set it to 180 degrees, use the following command line:

```
>>> analogWrite(PWM1A, 2.4, 20)
```

You will likely find that your motor has slightly different extremes than 0.5 ms and 2.4 ms, so you should use the interpreter to find the lowest and highest values that make the motor move by trial and error and take note of them.

To drive a servo motor from `Adafruit_BBIO`, you'll need to convert the pulse widths to percentages. As we just calculated, with a frequency of 50 Hz, the period of each cycle will be 20 ms. As the duty cycle is the percentage of the period during which the output is in a high state, we can calculate it by dividing the desired pulse width by the period, for example, *0.5 ms / 20 ms = 0.025*. This will give us a value in the range of 0–1, so we then just need to multiply by 100 to get a percentage for `PWM`. `set_duty_cycle()`. As an example, here's a program that will alternate the motor between its minimum and maximum rotation angles:

```
import time
from Adafruit_BBIO import PWM
```

```
servo_pin = "P9_14"
servo_min = 100*0.5/20.0
servo_max = 100*2.4/20.0

PWM.start(servo_pin, 0, 50)

try:
  while True:
    PWM.set_duty_cycle(servo_pin, servo_min)
    time.sleep(2)
    PWM.set_duty_cycle(servo_pin, servo_max)
    time.sleep(2)
except KeyboardInterrupt:
  PWM.cleanup()
```

Again, you will most likely need to replace the `0.5` and `2.4` values with the extremes you found for your motor.

PyBBIO also includes a library specifically for servo motors, so you don't actually need to deal with changing the frequency and figuring out the duty cycles for the angles you want to set them to. This is provided as a `Servo` class in the `bbio.libraries.Servo` module, as shown in the following code;

```
from bbio import *
from bbio.libraries.Servo import Servo

motor = Servo(PWM1A)

def setup():
    pass

def loop():
    for i in range(0, 180):
        motor.write(i)
    for i in range(180, 0, -1):
        motor.write(i)

run(setup, loop)
```

When you run this example, you should see your servo motor sweep back and forth. If you found that you have different minimum and maximum pulse widths than the default 0.5 ms and 2.4 ms, you can specify them when you instantiate the `Servo()` object, for example:

```
motor = Servo(servo_pin, min_ms=0.8, max_ms=2.2)
```

ADC

The BeagleBone has 7 available inputs to its analog-to-digital converter (refer to *Appendix A, The BeagleBone Black Pinout* to see which pins support analog inputs). The ADC can approximate voltages at each of these pins between 0 V and 1.8 V. As mentioned in *Chapter 1, Before We Begin*, putting voltages greater than 1.8 V on any of the ADC's input pins will damage your BeagleBone. That doesn't mean we can't measure higher voltages with it, we just need some external circuitry to do so.

Voltage divider

The simplest method for measuring voltages greater than 1.8 V is to use a voltage divider, which is simply composed of two resistors in a series between your voltage source and 0 V, with the output being the node between them:

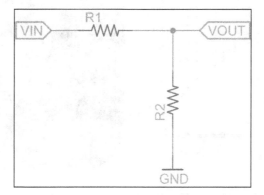

The output voltage is calculated by the formula $R2 / (R1 + R2) * VIN$. So if VIN is 3.3 V and both resistors are 10 kΩ, then VOUT will be 1.65 V, and if VIN is 5 V, R1 is 10 kΩ, and R2 is 5 kΩ, then VOUT will be 1.67 V. So with those two examples, we could easily monitor the BeagleBone's 5 V and 3.3 V supplies using the on board ADC, and we could simply compensate for the divider in software by multiplying the measured voltages by two and three respectively. Let's give it a try.

For this, you will need:

- Breadboard
- 3x 10 kΩ resistor
- 1x 4.7 kΩ resistor
- Jumper wires

Use two of the 10 kΩ resistors to divide the 3.3 V supply by two and then wire that into the AIN4 ADC input (P9.33), and use the other 10 kΩ and 4.7 kΩ resistors to divide the 5 V supply and wire that to the AIN6 ADC input (P9.35). As mentioned earlier, using 10 kΩ and 5 kΩ resistors will divide the 5 V supply by 3, but 5 kΩ is not a standard resistor value so we'll use 4.7 kΩ instead. Wire up the circuit like so:

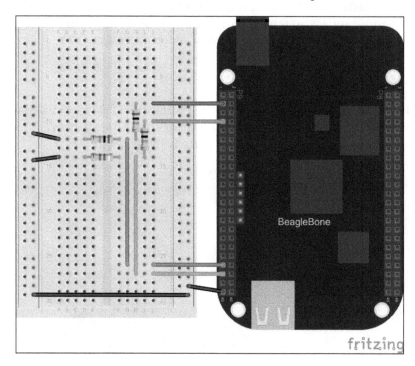

Now hop into the Python interactive interpreter, and let's try reading the voltages:

```
>>> from bbio import *
>>> analogRead(AIN4)
1692
```

The return value of `analogRead()` will be the voltage in millivolts present on the given analog input pin. You can convert this to volts with the PyBBIO's `inVolts()` function. Then you just multiply the voltage appropriately to get the voltage present on the input of the voltage divider:

```
from bbio import *

v_5v = inVolts(analogRead(AIN5)) * (4.7 + 10)/4.7
v_3v3 = inVolts(analogRead(AIN4)) * 2.0
```

```
print "5V input = {:0.2f}".format(v_5v)
print "3.3V supply = {:0.2f}".format(v_3v3)
```

In PyBBIO the ADC is automatically enabled with a Device Tree overlay the first time you call `analogRead()`. `Adafruit_BBIO` also loads the ADC overlay for you, but you have to explicitly call the `ADC.setup()` function to tell it to do so:

```
from Adafruit_BBIO import ADC

ADC.setup()
v_5v = 1.8 * ADC.read("P9_35") * (10 + 4.7)/4.7
v_3v3 = 1.8 * ADC.read("P9_33") * 2.0
print "5V input = {:0.2f}".format(v_5v)
print "3.3V supply = {:0.2f}".format(v_3v3)
```

Also, as you can see, we're multiplying the value by `1.8`. This is because the `ADC.read()` function of `Adafruit_BBIO` returns the value as a ratio of the ADC's 1.8 V reference voltage. Multiplying the returned value by `1.8` gives us the measured voltage in volts.

 Some versions of the Cloud9 IDE will lose the first line printed by your program in the output console. This can be easily worked around by inserting a single print statement at the top of your program.

The voltage divider is great for measuring DC supplies and the buffered outputs of powered sensors, but because it is just a simple resistive network, it doesn't play well with other devices and circuits that have series resistances in the same order of magnitude. For example, you might want to monitor the current that your LED is drawing from one of the circuits, as we did in *Chapter 3, Digital Outputs*.

Voltage follower

As mentioned earlier, the voltage follower doesn't work well when the input is coming from another circuit with low resistances in its path (known as low impedance outputs), as they will form a more complex resistor network and affect the output voltage. One way to avoid this problem is to use a voltage follower (or buffer) to isolate the two circuits.

There are a number of ways to make voltage followers, but we'll use one of the simplest, which is made with just a single stage of an operational amplifier (or op-amp), as shown in the following schematic:

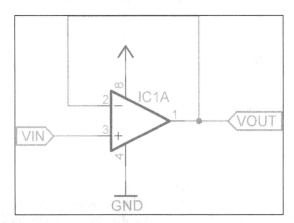

The op-amp's connections in the schematic are labeled as per the standard pinout for an 8-pin dual op-amp, which is one of the most common op-amp packages. The pin numbers follow the standard numbering for **dual in-line package** (**DIP**) integrated circuits, where the pins are numbered from 1 onwards in a U pattern starting at the top left (pin 1 is typically marked by a dot and/or half circle), as seen in the image:

The basic idea of the voltage follower is that it has high input impedance, meaning that there is a very large resistance between the input and ground, and it has low output impedance, meaning that there is a very low resistance in a series with the output. This means that we can put just about anything on the input side, and a voltage divider on the output side won't interfere with it. Let's look at a circuit that uses a voltage follower.

For this, you will need:

- Breadboard
- 1x CdS photocell (also known as photoresistor / light-dependant resistor / LDR)
- 2x 10 kΩ resistor
- 1x 4.7 kΩ resistor
- 1x LM358 (or similar rail-to-rail op-amp)
- Jumper wires

We will be wiring up the op-amp as shown in the schematic:

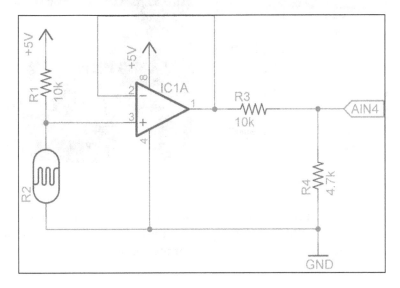

In this circuit, we're using a photocell (**R2**), which is just a resistor whose resistance varies with light. If there is a voltage across a photocell and its resistance changes with the light, the current passing through the photocell will also change. The BeagleBone's ADC can only measure voltages, so we use a 10 kΩ resistor (**R1**) to create a voltage that varies with the light (it's another voltage divider). This photocell circuit is being powered by a higher voltage than the ADC's 1.8 V maximum, so we need to divide the voltage from the sensor. The voltage follower made with the LM358 op-amp isolates the two circuits so they don't interfere with each other. Let's have a look at the following figure:

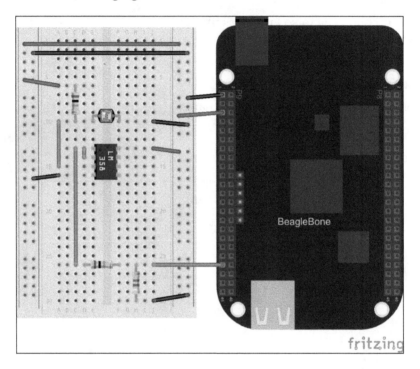

Wire up the circuit and run this program to print the voltage across the photocell, and you should see the voltage changing as you move your hand in front of the sensor or shine a light on it. Let's have a look at the following code:

```
from bbio import *

ldr_pin = AIN4

def setup():
```

```
    pass

def loop():
    vin = inVolts(analogRead(ldr_pin))
    vin *= (10 + 4.7)/4.7
    print "voltage across LDR: {:0.2f}V".format(vin)
    delay(500)

run(setup, loop)
```

You could do the same in `Adafruit_BBIO` with the following code:

```
import time
import Adafruit_BBIO.ADC as ADC

ADC.setup()
while True:
    vin = 1.8 * ADC.read("P9_33")
    vin *= (10 + 4.7)/4.7
    print "voltage across LDR: {:0.2f}V".format(vin)
    time.sleep(0.5)
```

Your first robot

You've now learned enough to make a simple robot. Its purpose is to always be looking at the closest object. OK, it's not the most exciting robot, but it's a great demo of how you can combine what you've learned about the PWM and ADC subsystems.

For this, you will need:

- Breadboard
- 1x Sharp IR proximity sensor
- 1x micro servo motor
- 3x 1 kΩ resistor
- 1x 0.1 µF capacitor
- Jumper wires

Wire up the circuit on your breadboard, as shown in the figure:

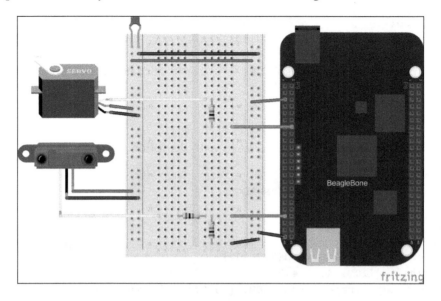

The Sharp IR proximity sensor contains an infrared LED, an infrared detector, and some circuitry to drive them. The detector measures the amount of infrared light that is reflected back from whatever object is in front of it, which will vary depending on how close the object is, and a voltage is generated on the output which corresponds to the distance. It requires a 5 V supply to operate, and the output voltage can exceed 3 V. Therefore, a voltage divider is used to not exceed the ADC's 1.8 V maximum. The sensor has a high impedance output from its on board amplifier, so we can get away without a voltage follower.

Wire up the circuit, attach the proximity sensor to the servo motor, and the servo motor to a flat surface, as shown in the following image:

When the program starts up, it will scan across the full range of the motor and record the measured distances along the way. It will then rotate the motor back to the position where the least distance was measured. It will then stay there until the object it's looking at moves, then it will start the process over. Let's have a look at the following code:

```python
from bbio import *
from bbio.libraries.Servo import Servo

range_pin = AIN0
servo_pin = PWM1A

servo = Servo(min_ms=0.81, max_ms=1.99)

def setup():
    servo.attach(servo_pin)

def loop():
    max_v_in = 0
    angle = 0
    for i in range(0, 180):
        servo.write(i)
        delay(1)
        v_in = analogRead(range_pin)
        if v_in > max_v_in:
            max_v_in = v_in
            angle = i
    servo.write(angle)
    delay(500)
    while (abs(max_v_in - analogRead(range_pin)) < 200):
        delay(100)

run(setup, loop)
```

The 1 millisecond delay in the scan is there to ensure the motor has had time to reach the set location before measuring the distance. The greater the sensor's output voltage, the closer the object that it's looking at it. Whenever we see a higher voltage than we have previously during a scan, we save the measured voltage and angle. That way, once the scan has finished, we know that the angle saved was the angle at which the closest object was detected. The 500 ms delay once again ensures that the motor has reached that angle, then the `while` loop holds the motor there until the voltage measured has changed by at least 200 mV. If we were to simply wait until the voltage changed at all, then any amount of noise on the input (which is inevitable) would cause it to rescan. The 100 ms delay in the `while` loop keeps the program from hogging the CPU while it's waiting.

Summary

In this chapter, you learned how to use the pulse width modulation and analog-to-digital converter subsystems with PyBBIO and Adafruit_BBIO. You learned how to use PWM to set the brightness of LEDs and drive servo motors. You also learned how to measure voltages with the ADC, and how to use voltage dividers and buffers to measure voltages greater than 1.8 V.

In the next chapter, you will learn to incorporate buttons and potentiometers into your circuits to receive user input.

5
User Input

In this chapter, you will learn how to let your BeagleBone programs receive user input through external hardware. We will cover the following topics:

- Buttons
- Potentiometers

Buttons

A button is one of the simplest input devices you can connect to your BeagleBone. To sense the state of a button, we only need to use a single GPIO pin configured as an input. We haven't used a GPIO input yet, so let's take a look at a simple example first.

For this circuit, you will need:

- Breadboard
- 1x tactile switches
- 1x 10 kΩ resistors
- Jumper wires

A tactile switch is a type of momentary push button, meaning that it is only engaged while it is held down and returns to its default state when released. They are widely available from stores such as Adafruit and SparkFun, and it is also one of the more breadboard-friendly types of switches. Depending on the variety of tactile switch, it might require straightening the pins with a pair of pliers to get it to lock into your breadboard. Wire the switch to GPIO0_30 (P9.11), as shown in the figure:

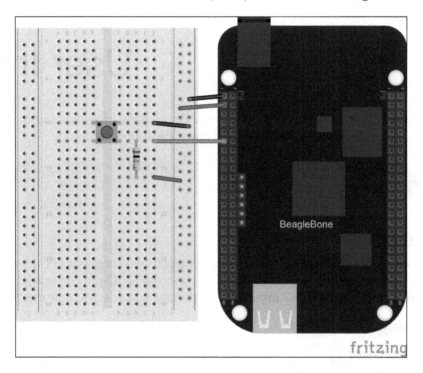

Now run the following code and press the button; you should see a value of 0 normally and 1 when you press the button:

```python
from bbio import *

SW_PIN = GPIO0_30

def setup():
  pinMode(SW_PIN, INPUT)

def loop():
  print "switch state:", digitalRead(SW_PIN)
  delay(250)

run(setup, loop)
```

To do the same in `Adafruit_BBIO`, we'll first need to configure the pin as an input, as shown in the following code:

```
# config-pin P9_11 in
```

 Remember, you'll need to first load the universal cape overlay as described in *Chapter 3, Digital Outputs*, before using a config-pin.

You can then use `GPIO.input()` to read the pin state:

```
from Adafruit_BBIO import GPIO
import time

GPIO.setup("P9_11", GPIO.IN)

while True:
print "switch state:", GPIO.input("P9_11")
time.sleep(0.25)
```

Pull-up/pull-down resistors

So what's the resistor in the preceding circuit for? Let's think about what would happen without the resistor. When you press the button, the two sets of pins are shorted together, and therefore, the GPIO input is connected to ground. The 0 V ground level is read by the GPIO module as a logical low, and 0 is returned. When the button is not pressed, the two sets of pins are disconnected from each other, leaving the GPIO input disconnected, or floating. In this floating state, external electric fields can induce voltages on the GPIO input, especially with the external wire connecting it to the switch acting as an antenna. These induced voltages might or might not cross the GPIO module's low-high threshold. So leaving a GPIO input in a floating state will result in unpredictable readings.

We can easily avoid leaving the GPIO input floating when connecting a switch by adding a single resistor. In the preceding circuit, when the button is pressed the GPIO input is still connected directly to ground, and therefore the voltage is still 0 and a low value is read. When not pressed, the GPIO input is connected to 3.3 V, and since the input has much higher impedance than the 10 kΩ of the resistor, the voltage on the input is 3.3 V and high value is read. This is called a pull-up resistor, because this is pulling the input up to 3.3 V. The circuit can also be reversed, where the switch connects the input to 3.3 V and the resistor pulls it down to 0 V when not pressed, in which case it is called a pull-down resistor.

The value of the pull resistor is not crucial, but you typically want something in the range of 1 kΩ-100 kΩ. If the value is very low, then there can be a large amount of current flowing through it when the switch is engaged. If the value is very high, it can create a voltage divider with the input impedance of the GPIO module when the switch is not engaged, potentially dividing the voltage down below the LOW-HIGH threshold. 10 kΩ is a good choice for most applications.

The GPIO modules in the BeagleBone's processor also include configurable pull-up and pull-down resistors, and PyBBIO allows you to use them in place of external resistors. First, wire up the tactile switch without any pull resistor.

For this circuit, you will need:

- Breadboard
- 1x tactile switches
- Jumper wires

The connection is shown in the following figure:

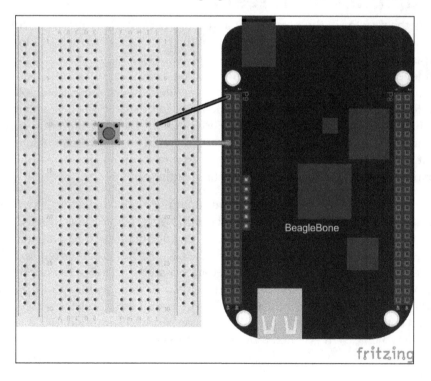

Then we just need to enable the internal pull-up resistor when we call the `pinMode()` function, as shown in the following code:

```
from bbio import *

SW_PIN = GPIO0_30

def setup():
    pinMode(SW_PIN, INPUT, PULLUP)

def loop():
    print "switch state:", digitalRead(SW_PIN)
    delay(250)

run(setup, loop)
```

To use the internal pull-down resistor, you can use the PULLDOWN keyword instead.

The pull-up and pull-down resistors are part of the pin multiplexing subsystem, and therefore, must be set through the device tree. PyBBIO does this with its custom overlays, but if you're using `Adafruit_BBIO`, you can still enable pull-up and pull-down resistors with `config-pin`. To enable a pull-up resistor, append a plus sign to the `in` option, as shown in the following code:

```
# config-pin P9_11 in+
```

Append a minus sign for a pull-down resistor:

```
# config-pin P9_11 in-
```

Polling

One technique for reading buttons is called polling, where a program repeatedly reads the input state fast enough to catch button presses. Let's take a look at an example of this. First, wire up two tactile switches, this time to GPIO0_30 (P9.11) and GPIO3_15 (P9.29).

For this circuit, you will need:

- Breadboard
- 2x tactile switches
- 2x 10 kΩ resistors
- Jumper wires

Place the buttons on your breadboard, as shown in the diagram:

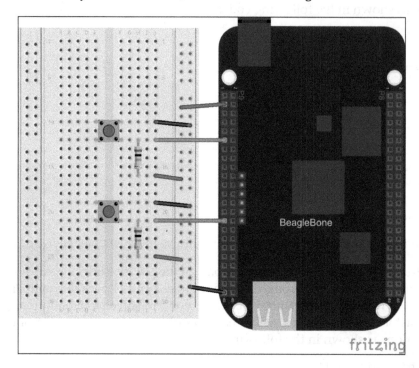

Try out the following program as an example:

```
from bbio import *

UP_SW = GPIO0_30
DOWN_SW = GPIO3_15

set_value = 50
min_value = 0
max_value = 100

def setup():
    pinMode(UP_SW, INPUT)
    pinMode(DOWN_SW, INPUT)

def loop():
    global set_value
    if (not digitalRead(UP_SW) and set_value < max_value):
        set_value += 1
```

```
        print "value set to {:d}".format(set_value)
    if (not digitalRead(DOWN_SW) and set_value > min_value):
        set_value -= 1
        print "value set to {:d}".format(set_value)
    delay(100)

run(setup, loop)
```

When you run it, you should see it responding to your button presses by incrementing and decrementing the global set_value variable. Set a delay of 100 in the loop() function; because the program is continually reading the button states each time through the loop, the delay helps to prevent it from registering many button presses at once (don't take my word for it, try running the program without it). That delay can become a problem when you start doing other tasks in your program, as it eats up processing time. So let's look at a couple other ways to handle this.

The first technique is to ignore each button for a set amount of time after the first push is detected, as shown in the following code:

```
from bbio import *

UP_SW    = GPIO0_30
DOWN_SW  = GPIO3_15

DEBOUNCE_MS = 250
last_up_press = -DEBOUNCE_MS
last_down_press = -DEBOUNCE_MS

set_value = 50
min_value = 0
max_value = 100

def setup():
    pinMode(UP_SW, INPUT)
    pinMode(DOWN_SW, INPUT)

def loop():
    global set_value, last_up_press, last_down_press
    now = millis()
    if (not digitalRead(UP_SW) and set_value < max_value):
        if (now - last_up_press >= DEBOUNCE_MS):
            set_value += 1
            print "value set to {:d}".format(set_value)
```

```
                last_up_press = now
    if (not digitalRead(DOWN_SW) and set_value > min_value):
        if (now - last_down_press >= DEBOUNCE_MS):
            set_value -= 1
            print "value set to {:d}".format(set_value)
            last_down_press = now
    delay(10)


run(setup, loop)
```

So, in this case, we're using the PyBBIO's `millis()` function, which returns the number of milliseconds that have elapsed since the program started running, to compare each LOW GPIO reading to the time of the last registered button press for that input. The LOW level is only registered as a button press if at least the configured number of milliseconds have passed.

> We've used the variable name DEBOUNCE_MS because this is equivalent to a simple button debouncing. When a button is pressed, the metal contacts inside it tend to bounce off each other a few times before making solid contact, and debouncing is used to prevent this from causing multiple button press events. Python running in GNU/Linux on the BeagleBone doesn't run fast enough to pick up button bounce, but this is still the same technique nonetheless.

Another strategy is to completely ignore a pressed button until it has been released. Let's take a look at the following code:

```
from bbio import *

UP_SW   = GPIO0_30
DOWN_SW = GPIO3_15

up_pressed = False
down_pressed = False

set_value = 50
min_value = 0
max_value = 100

def setup():
    pinMode(UP_SW, INPUT)
```

```
    pinMode(DOWN_SW, INPUT)

def loop():
    global set_value, up_pressed, down_pressed
    now = millis()
    if (not digitalRead(UP_SW) and set_value < max_value):
        if (not up_pressed):
          set_value += 1
          print "value set to {}".format(set_value)
          up_pressed = True
    else: up_pressed = False
    if not (digitalRead(DOWN_SW) and set_value > min_value):
        if (not down_pressed):
            set_value -= 1
            print "value set to {}".format(set_value)
            down_pressed = True
    else: down_pressed = False
    delay(10)

run(setup, loop)
```

What's nice about this technique is that you can repeatedly press the buttons as fast as you'd like without having the forced delay between presses. Of course, there are plenty of other techniques of cleaning up button presses, including different combinations of the ones here.

Before we continue, let's take the example we've been working on one step further, and actually make it do something. Start by adding the NPN LED driving circuit we looked at in *Chapter 3*, *Digital Outputs*, to PWM1A (P9.16). The external pull-up resistors have been removed here to make more space on the breadboard.

For this circuit, you will need:

- Breadboard
- 2x tactile switches
- 1x 5 mm LED
- 1x 4.7 kΩ resistor
- 1x 68 Ω resistor
- 1x 2N3904 NPN transistor
- Jumper wires

Wire the buttons on your breadboard, as shown in the figure:

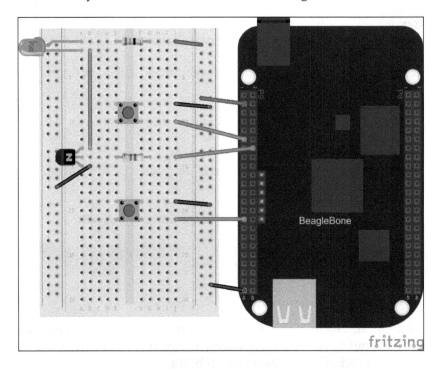

With just a few additions, we can make the two-button-example control the brightness of the LED, as shown in the following code:

```
from bbio import *

UP_SW    = GPIO0_30
DOWN_SW  = GPIO3_15
LED      = PWM1A

DEBOUNCE_MS = 250
last_up_press = -DEBOUNCE_MS
last_down_press = -DEBOUNCE_MS

set_value = 50
min_value = 0
max_value = 100
```

```
    increment = 5

def setup():
    pinMode(UP_SW, INPUT, PULLUP)
    pinMode(DOWN_SW, INPUT, PULLUP)
    analogWrite(LED, set_value, 100)

def loop():
    global set_value, last_up_press, last_down_press
    now = millis()
    value_changed = False
    if (not digitalRead(UP_SW) and
        set_value <= max_value-increment):
        if (now - last_up_press >= DEBOUNCE_MS):
            set_value += increment
            print "value set to {:%i}".format( % set_value)
            last_up_press = now
            value_changed = True
    if (not digitalRead(DOWN_SW) and
        set_value >= min_value+increment):
        if (now - last_down_press >= DEBOUNCE_MS):
            set_value -= increment
            print "value set to {:i}".format(set_value)
            last_down_press = now
            value_changed = True

    if (value_changed): analogWrite(LED, set_value, 100)
    delay(10)

run(setup, loop)
```

One of the additions is the global `increment` variable, which lets you set the amount each button press changes the duty cycle by; that way you don't have to press it a hundred times to go from a 0 to 100 percent duty cycle. Also added is the `value_changed` variable, which ensures that the PWM module is only being reconfigured when a change has been requested by way of a button press. Without this, the value would always be set every 10 ms; and each time it is set, there is a slight interruption in the PWM output while the new value is taking effect, which would cause a noticeable flicker on the LED.

Interrupts

Polling buttons can be troublesome when your program has to do other work at the same time. One alternative is to use what's called interrupts. Like most modern microcontrollers and microprocessors, the BeagleBone's processor supports GPIO input interrupts. They can trigger the processor to jump to a particular location in its program memory when it detects a certain state on a GPIO input. The supported states are typically rising and falling edges (that is, the transitions between logic levels), and low or high levels themselves. The Linux kernel on the BeagleBone is able to receive these interrupt signals and generate a change to a special file if configured to do so. A user space process (as opposed to a kernel space process, like a kernel driver) can then monitor the said file, and can call a locally defined callback function when it detects a change. That might sound a bit complicated, but it's pretty straightforward to use interrupts in PyBBIO, especially if you've written any event-driven code before. Let's take a look at what the LED brightness control program might look like using interrupts instead of polling, as shown in the following code:

```python
from bbio import *

UP_SW    = GPIO0_30
DOWN_SW  = GPIO3_15
LED      = PWM1A

DEBOUNCE_MS = 250
last_up_press = -DEBOUNCE_MS
last_down_press = -DEBOUNCE_MS
value_changed = False

set_value = 50
min_value = 0
max_value = 100
increment = 5

def upHandler():
    global set_value, last_up_press, value_changed
    now = millis()
    if (now - last_up_press < DEBOUNCE_MS): return
    if (set_value <= max_value-increment):
        set_value += increment
        print "value set to {:i}".format(set_value)
        last_up_press = now
```

```
        value_changed = True

def downHandler():
    global set_value, last_down_press, value_changed
    now = millis()
    if (now - last_down_press < DEBOUNCE_MS): return
    if (set_value >= min_value+increment):
        set_value -= increment
        print "value set to {:i}".format(set_value)
        last_down_press = now
        value_changed = True

def setup():
    pinMode(UP_SW, INPUT, PULLUP)
    pinMode(DOWN_SW, INPUT, PULLUP)
    attachInterrupt(UP_SW, upHandler, FALLING)
    attachInterrupt(DOWN_SW, downHandler, FALLING)
    analogWrite(LED, set_value, 100)

def loop():
    global value_changed
    if (value_changed):
        analogWrite(LED, set_value, 100)
        value_changed = False
    delay(10)

run(setup, loop)
```

Notice how the main loop is completely free to do any additional work that might be required by your program.

`Adafruit_BBIO` doesn't implement interrupt `callback` functions like PyBBIO does, but it does have two options to receive interrupt signals. The first is the blocking `wait_for_edge()` function, which blocks the program until the specified edge is detected. For example, we could wait for a button press on GPIO0_30 (the preceding circuit will work). Let's take a look at the following code:

```
from Adafruit_BBIO import GPIO

button = "P9_11"
GPIO.setup(button, GPIO.IN)
GPIO.wait_for_edge(button, GPIO.FALLING)
print "Button pressed!"
```

The other option is to tell `Adafruit_BBIO` to detect a particular edge in the background, then routinely ask it if it has been detected. Let's take a look at the following code:

```
from Adafruit_BBIO import GPIO
import time

button = "P9_11"
GPIO.setup(button, GPIO.IN)
GPIO.add_event_detect(button, GPIO.FALLING)

while True:
    if GPIO.event_detected(button):
        print "Button pressed!"
    time.sleep(1)
```

This won't necessarily allow you to respond to interrupts as quickly as possible, but it will at least guarantee that your program won't miss any input signals while it's taking care of other tasks.

In both cases, you'll want to first enable the pull-up resistor, as shown in the following code:

```
# config-pin P9_11 in+
```

Potentiometers

Another option for user input is to use the ADC to read the position of a potentiometer. Let's revisit some of the things you learned in *Chapter 4, PWM and ADC Subsystems*, to make our program a bit more interesting.

For this circuit, you will need:

- Breadboard
- 2x potentiometers
- 1x 5 mm LED
- 1x CdS photocell (also known as photoresistor / light-dependant resistor / LDR)

- 2x 10 kΩ resistor

- 1x 4.7 kΩ resistor

- 1x 68 Ω resistor

- 1x 2N3904 NPN transistor

- 1x LM358 (or similar rail-to-rail op-amp)

- Jumper wires

Put it all together on your breadboard, as shown in the figure:

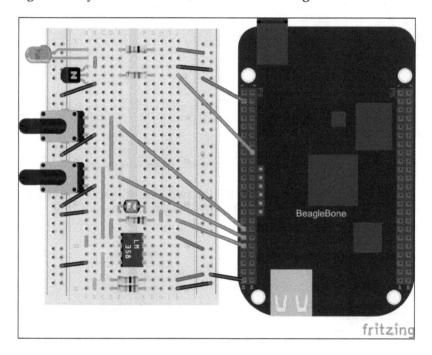

This circuit might look a lot more complicated than what we've done so far, but really it's just a combination of a few of the earlier circuits. The only difference is the configuration of the op-amp.

Here it is being used to buffer the output of a 2:1 voltage divider across the 3.3 V rail, which creates a 1.65 V reference voltage. Let's take a look at the following diagram:

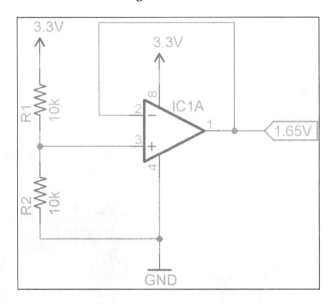

This 1.65 V reference is then being used by the two potentiometers and the photocell. This is yet another solution for the 1.8 V limit of the BeagleBone's ADC, as discussed in *Chapter 4, PWM and ADC Subsystems*.

Now, take a look at the example program:

```
from bbio import *

BRIGHTNESS = AIN4
THRESHOLD   = AIN6
LDR         = AIN2
LED         = PWM1A

HYSTERESIS = 50

brightness = 0
light_on = False

def setup():
    analogWrite(LED, 0)

def loop():
    global brightness, light_on.
```

```
adc_max = 3300/2
value_changed = False
value = analogRead(BRIGHTNESS)
percent = int(100 * value/adc_max)
if (percent > 100): percent = 100
if (percent < 0): percent = 0
if (percent != brightness):
    brightness = percent
    value_changed = True

threshold = analogRead(THRESHOLD)
light = analogRead(LDR)
force_update = False
if (light >= threshold+HYSTERESIS):
    if (not light_on): force_update = True
    light_on = True
elif (light <= threshold-HYSTERESIS):
    if (light_on): force_update = True
    light_on = False

if (light_on):
    if (value_changed or force_update):
        analogWrite(LED, brightness, 100)
elif (force_update):
    analogWrite(LED, 0, 100)
delay(10)

run(setup, loop)
```

Like the buttons before, the potentiometer connected to AIN4 (P9.33) controls the brightness of the LED, from 0 percent to 100 percent. The value from the second potentiometer is compared to the value from the photocell voltage divider. If the photocell voltage is greater, the light is turned on at the set brightness; otherwise, it is turned off. It's your very own variable brightness night light. It might not seem that exciting, but it's the first application we've looked at that's not simply a demonstration of one particular thing, but is actually a working, somewhat-practical object.

This circuit includes some hysteresis. Try setting the HYSTERESIS variable to 0 and see what happens as you approach the threshold by slowly bringing your finger towards the photocell. At a certain point, you should see the LED start to quickly flash on and off. This is because there is a certain amount of noise, both in the light in the room and in the BeagleBone's power supply and ADC, which causes the readings to jump above and below the threshold. This behavior is avoided by adding some hysteresis to the control loop as in this example program.

Summary

In this chapter, you learned the basics of using buttons and potentiometers to generate user input in your programs. We looked at both synchronous polling and interrupt-based input. We also looked at some concepts like debouncing and hysteresis to help receive clean input signals. Finally, you made a variable brightness night light.

In the next chapter, we'll take a look at some more ways of providing output to the user, other than printing text to the terminal.

6
Program Output

In this chapter, you will learn different ways of providing output from your BeagleBone programs. We will cover the following topics:

- LED displays
    - LED bar graphs
    - 7-segment displays
    - LED matrixes

- SMTP
    - E-mail
    - Text messages

- Character LCDs

LED displays

One of the simplest forms of hardware output that we can add to a program is an LED attached to a GPIO pin. We've already blinked LEDs, but not in a way that conveyed any sort of meaningful information; so first things first, we'll need something to communicate to the user. Here's a simple program that uses **Internet Message Access Protocol (IMAP)** to login to your email account and retrieve the number of unread messages in your inbox. Save it as a new file called `email_counter.py`, either in Cloud9 or your editor of choice over SSH, filling in the IMAP details for your account, as shown in the following code:

```
import imaplib

IMAP_host = "imap.gmail.com"
IMAP_email = "username@gmail.com"
```

```
IMAP_pass = "password"

email = imaplib.IMAP4_SSL(IMAP_host)

def connect():
    email.login(IMAP_email, IMAP_pass)

def disconnect():
    email.close()
    email.logout()

def get_num_emails():
    email.select("INBOX")
    ret, data = email.search(None, "UNSEEN")
    return len(data[0].split())
```

 IMAP is a standard protocol for e-mail clients, so no matter who your e-mail provider is, you should be able to find the appropriate IMAP details, either through their own official instructions or through a web search.

Now hook up the LED and NPN transistor circuit we've used in previous chapters; in this example, we will use GPIO1_28, which is on pin P9.12. This PyBBIO program will use email_counter.py to periodically retrieve the number of e-mails, and will light the LED if they exceed the indicate_above threshold, as shown in the following code:

```
from bbio import *
import email_counter

# Light LED if greater than this many unread emails:
indicate_above = 1

led_pin = GPIO1_28

def setup():
    pinMode(led_pin, OUTPUT)
    digitalWrite(led_pin, LOW)
    email_counter.connect()
    addToCleanup(email_counter.disconnect)

def loop():
    n_email = email_counter.get_num_emails()
```

```
    if (n_email > indicate_above): digitalWrite(led_pin, HIGH)
    else: digitalWrite(led_pin, LOW)
    delay(5000)

run(setup, loop)
```

 When you tell Python to import something, it first looks for a module (a single .py file) or package (a directory containing a __init__. py file) in the same directory as the file with the import statement. If it can't find it there, it then searches the Python path (# python -c "import sys; print sys.path"). Make sure that email_ counter.py is saved in the same directory as your program so that Python is able to find and import it.

If you want to make that boring LED indicator a bit more exciting, you can drive it from a PWM pin instead and generate a heartbeat effect, instead of just lighting it at full brightness:

```
from bbio import *
import email_counter, threading

# Light LED if greater than this many unread emails:
indicate_above = 0
led = PWM1A # P9.14

heartbeat_enabled = 0

def do_heartbeat():
  while True:
    if (heartbeat_enabled):
      for i in range(0, 100):
        analogWrite(PWM1A, i, 100)
        delay(10)
        for i in range(100, 0, -1):
          analogWrite(PWM1A, i, 100)
          delay(10)
    else:
      analogWrite(PWM1A, 0)
      delay(700)

def setup():
  email_counter.connect()
  addToCleanup(email_counter.disconnect)
  t = threading.Thread(target=do_heartbeat)
```

```
      t.daemon = True
      t.start()

  def loop():
    global heartbeat_enabled
    n_email = email_counter.get_num_emails()
    if (n_email > indicate_above): heartbeat_enabled = 1
    else: heartbeat_enabled = 0
    delay(5000)

  run(setup, loop)
```

This program is also a good example of using Python's threading to help make your hardware interfacing more asynchronous.

LED bar graphs

Okay, a single LED is not that exciting, so let's add some more. Thanks to the BeagleBone's huge number of GPIO pins, it's no problem to drive a 10-segment LED bar graph, like the ones sold at Adafruit (for example, `https://www.adafruit.com/products/1816`). Remember that each of the BeagleBone's GPIO pins can only supply a maximum current of 4-6 mA. Luckily, the bar graphs from Adafruit use high efficiency LEDs, and when driven from 3.3 V with a series 330 Ω resistor, they draw under 2 mA, which means they are safe to drive directly from the GPIO pins. If using a different bar graph, you should go through the calculations to make sure it won't be drawing too much current.

For this circuit, you will need:

- Breadboard
- 1x 10 segment LED bar graph
- 10x 330 Ω resistors
- Jumper wires

The connection is shown in the following figure:

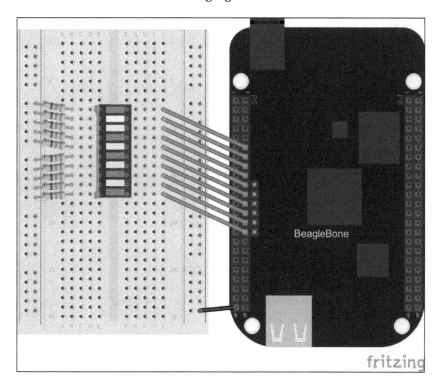

Now, let's modify the previous program a bit to use the bar graph as an indication of the number of unread e-mails. We can put all the GPIO pins in a list in order to help keep the code a bit cleaner:

```
from bbio import *
import email_counter

# Bar graph will be full if this many emails or more are unread:
n_emails_full = 10

graph_pins = [
    GPIO1_28, # P9.12
    GPIO1_18, # P9.14
    GPIO1_19, # P9.16
    GPIO0_4,  # P9.18
    GPIO0_12, # P9.20
    GPIO0_2,  # P9.22
    GPIO0_15, # P9.24
    GPIO0_14, # P9.26
```

```
        GPIO3_17, # P9.28
        GPIO3_16  # P9.30
        ]

def set_level(level):
    for i in range(len(graph_pins)):
        if i < level: digitalWrite(graph_pins[i], HIGH)
        else: digitalWrite(graph_pins[i], LOW)

def setup():
    for pin in graph_pins:
        pinMode(pin, OUTPUT)
        digitalWrite(pin, LOW)
    email_counter.connect()
    addToCleanup(email_counter.disconnect)

def loop():
    n_email = email_counter.get_num_emails()
    max_level = len(graph_pins)
    level = float(n_email)/n_emails_full*max_level
    set_level(level)
    delay(5000)

run(setup, loop)
```

If you tend to have a large backlog of unread e-mails, you can increase n_emails_
full to change the scale of the bar graph.

7-segment displays

7-segment displays are the classic numeric indicators, named for their seven
separately lit segments that can be combined to form every digit from 0-9, as well
as many of the letters in the English alphabet. As each digit contains seven LEDs,
the number of pins required quickly becomes unreasonable and multiplexing
is required, where a small number of GPIO pins are used to quickly sequence
through the many LEDs. While this means that only a few LEDs are lit at a time, the
sequencing is done faster than the human eye can perceive, giving the illusion of all
the LEDs being lit at once.

While we could certainly multiplex a 7-segment display directly, Adafruit sells a convenient line of products for easily driving multiplexed LED displays using I2C (`https://www.adafruit.com/products/881`). We'll learn more about the I2C protocol later, but for now, all we need to know is that there's a data signal (SDA) and a clock signal (SCL), and on the BeagleBone, we'll be using P9.19 for SCL and P9.20 for SDA and connecting them to corresponding pins of the 7-segment display board. But first, you'll have to solder the display and connector onto the circuit board. Luckily, Adafruit provides a great tutorial for doing just that at `https://learn.adafruit.com/adafruit-led-backpack/0-dot-56-seven-segment-backpack`.

 This is the first device we've used that requires soldering. If you've never soldered before, there are plenty of great tutorials out there, such as by SparkFun at `https://learn.sparkfun.com/tutorials/how-to-solder---through-hole-soldering` and Adafruit at `https://learn.adafruit.com/adafruit-guide-excellent-soldering`.

We'll use a TMP36 temperature sensor in this circuit as well, so we'll have some temperature data to display. The TMP36 can be powered at 3.3 V, and it gives an output voltage that is linearly proportional to the temperature in centigrade, with a maximum output voltage of around 1.7 V. That makes it perfect for interfacing to the BeagleBone, as its output can be directly connected to the 1.8V ADC without a voltage divider.

For this circuit, you will need:

- Breadboard
- 1x Adafruit 7-segment display with I2C backpack
- 1x TMP36 temperature sensor
- 1x 0.1 µF capacitor
- Jumper wires

The connection is shown in the following figure:

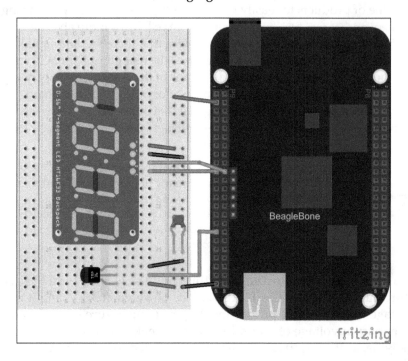

Adafruit provides a Python library for driving their I2C LED backpacks, so we'll start by opening a terminal and installing it along with its dependencies. Let's take a look at the following code:

```
# apt-get update
# apt-get install git python-imaging
# git clone
  https://github.com/adafruit/Adafruit_Python_LED_Backpack.git
# cd Adafruit_Python_LED_Backpack
# python setup.py install
```

Next, we'll need to figure out how to convert the voltage from the TMP36 into temperature. The datasheet specifies the output to be 10 mV/degrees Celsius, with an offset of 750 mV at 25 degrees Celsius. From this, we can derive the formula *tempC = (voltage - 750 mV) / 10 (mV/°C) + 25°C*, or using volts instead of millivolts *tempC = (voltage - 0.75 V) / 0.01 (V/°C) + 25°C*.

Now, let's put the pieces together and use the 7-segment display to show the current temperature, using `Adafruit_BBIO` this time:

```
From Adafruit_BBIO import ADC
from Adafruit_LED_Backpack import SevenSegment
import time

tmp36 = "P9_33" # AIN4

ADC.setup()
display = SevenSegment.SevenSegment()
display.begin()
display.set_colon(False)

def get_temp_c():
  v = ADC.read(tmp36)*1.8
  return (v - 0.75)*100.0 + 25

try:
  while True
    temp = int(get_temp_c())
    sign = '-' if temp < 0 else ' '
    temp_str = "{}{:2d}C".format(sign, abs(temp))
    display.clear()
    display.print_number_str(temp_str)
    display.write_display()
    time.sleep(1)
except KeyboardInterrupt:
    pass
```

I made the string formatting a bit more complicated than it needed to be because I wanted the minus sign to always be on the farthest left digit, even when displaying a one digit negative number.

The LED matrix

Let's look at one more form of multiplexed LED displays—the LED matrix. These are N x N arrays of LEDs, where typically, every LED can be individually lit through their multiplexing scheme. Adafruit's I2C LED backpacks include some LED matrixes, and in this case, we'll use the 8 x 8 single-color matrix, like the one available at https://www.adafruit.com/products/959. Once again, some soldering is required (tutorial at https://learn.adafruit.com/adafruit-led-backpack/0-8-8x8-matrix), then it can be wired to the BeagleBone just like the 7-segment display board was.

For this circuit, you will need:

- Breadboard
- 1x Adafruit 8 x 8 single-color LED matrix w/ I2C backpack
- Jumper wires

Connect the LED matrix like so:

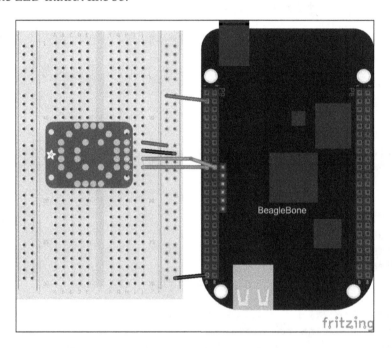

This time, let's look at doing some simple animation. First, open a terminal and install the psutil Python library, using the following command:

```
# pip install psutil
```

psutil provides functions to monitor system resources; in this case, we'll use it to create a scrolling graph of CPU usage:

```
import time, Image, ImageDraw, collections, psutil
from Adafruit_LED_Backpack import Matrix8x8

display = Matrix8x8.Matrix8x8()
display.begin()
display.clear()
display.write_display()
history = collections.deque([0]*8)
```

```
try:
    while True:
        load = psutil.cpu_percent(interval=2)
        height = load/100 * 8
        height = int(height + 0.5)
        if (height > 8): height = 8
        history.append(height)
        history.popleft()
        image = Image.new('1', (8, 8))
        draw = ImageDraw.Draw(image)
        for i in range(8):
            height = history[i]
            if (height > 0):
                draw.line((i,7,i,8-height), fill=255)
        display.set_image(image)
        display.write_display()
except KeyboardInterrupt:
    pass
```

Leave this running while you perform some other tasks on your BeagleBone, like running some other programs. You should see a nice scrolling bar graph. If you want to see the graph spike, you can run a program that will hog the CPU, for example, by repeatedly doing multiplication:

```
x = 100
while 1:
    x * x
```

SMTP

We've looked at various forms of displays that you can attach to your BeagleBone, but those are only useful when you're looking at it. If your BeagleBone is not accessible, for instance, it's monitoring something at your home while you're out, you might still need a way for it to send you information. One simple way to achieve this is to use **Simple Mail Transfer Protocol (SMTP)** to send e-mails from your BeagleBone. Save this code to a new file called email_sender.py by filling in your account's SMTP details:

```
import smtplib
from email.mime.text import MIMEText

SMTP_host = 'smtp.gmail.com'
SMTP_email = 'username@gmail.com'
SMTP_pass = 'password'
```

```
def send_email(to, subject, body):
    msg = MIMEText(body)
    msg['Subject'] = subject
    msg['From'] = SMTP_email
    msg['To'] = to
    server = smtplib.SMTP_SSL(SMTP_host)
    server.login(SMTP_email, SMTP_pass)
    server.sendmail(SMTP_email, to, msg.as_string())
```

 Just like with IMAP, to retrieve e-mails, SMTP is a standard protocol and is used by pretty much every e-mail provider, so you should be able to find the appropriate details for your account.

One possible application where you might want your BeagleBone to send you an e-mail is in a home security system. For this example, we'll use a PIR motion detector module, like the one from Adafruit at `https://www.adafruit.com/products/189`, to create a system that notifies you when motion is detected.

For this circuit, you will need:

- PIR motion detector module
- Matching cable

Hook up the PIR sensor as shown:

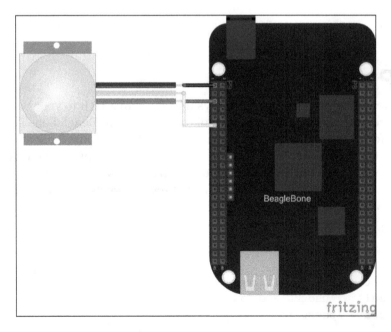

The module from Adafruit is great for two reasons, it comes with a cable, and its output signal is 3 V even though it is powered at 5 V. Pretty much all PIR motion detection modules work the same and have the same interface, but if you are using a different one, make sure to confirm with a multimeter that the output is 3 V, and use a voltage divider if it isn't.

The Adafruit module ship is configured to generate a low pulse when motion is detected, so we can wait for a falling edge on the GPIO pin it's connected to. There's a jumper on the module that lets you invert that signal, so there's a high pulse when motion is detected. Since we can detect both falling and rising edges, it doesn't really matter which way the output goes, just make sure to set the edge accordingly in the program:

```
import Adafruit_BBIO.GPIO as GPIO
import email_sender, time

PIR_pin = "P9_11" # GPIO0_30

email_address = "username@example.com"

def alert():
  email_sender.send_email(
    email_address,
    "BeagleBone motion detector",
    "Motion detected at {}".format(time.strftime("%x %X")))

GPIO.setup(PIR_pin, GPIO.IN)

while 1:
  GPIO.wait_for_edge(PIR_pin, GPIO.FALLING)
  alert()
```

We used `Adafruit_BBIO` for this example, taking advantage of the `GPIO.wait_for_edge()` function, which we looked at briefly in *Chapter 5, User Input*. This is great if you have nothing else to do in your program, as it lets you wait without using any extra system resources such as a `while` loop would, and then respond with as little latency as possible when the interrupt occurs.

Most cell phone providers have e-mail gateways to let you send text messages to numbers on their network via e-mail. There are many websites that provide lists of these gateways, such as `http://www.emailtextmessages.com/`. If you use your number and carrier's gateway instead of your e-mail address for the `email_address` variable, you can get the notifications from your BeagleBone as text messages instead.

Character LCD

We've looked at a few different types of LED displays, but because of the large size and spacing of their pixels they tend to be poor at conveying much information. When you want to display text, one of the simplest ways to do so is with a character LCD (liquid crystal display). These are rectangular displays typically consisting of 1, 2, or 4 lines of 8, 16, or 20 characters each, and are commonly used in radios and other low-cost electronics. Each character is typically made up of a matrix of 5 x 8 pixels, which is enough resolution to display any of the ASCII characters, along with some additional symbols.

For this example, I'm using a 2 x 16 character LCD. It will work with different sizes, but with a width of less than 16 characters, some of the text will be cut off. Character LCDs usually require a 5 V supply, but some companies such as SparkFun sell 3.3 V versions. Either version will work with the BeagleBone, just make sure to hook it up to the correct power supply. We'll also hook up a tactile switch and a TMP36 temperature sensor.

For this circuit, you will need:

- Breadboard
- 1x 16 x 2 character LCD
- 1x potentiometer (value not critical, 1 kΩ - 10 kΩ recommended)
- 1x tactile switch
- 1x TMP36 temperature sensor
- 1x 0.1µF capacitor
- Jumper wires

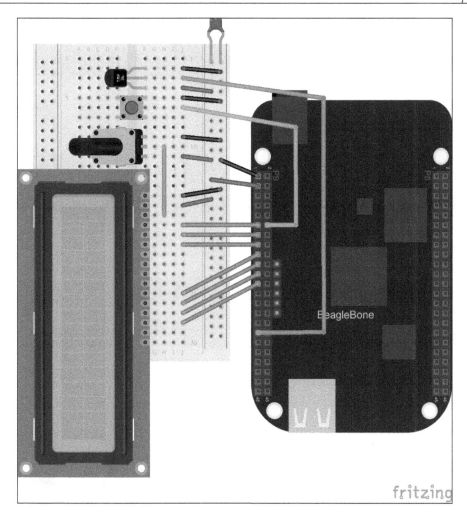

In this example, the LCD is used to display the CPU and TMP36 temperatures, the percentage of CPU and memory resources currently being used, and the number of network packets that have been sent and received. That's way too much information to display on the screen all at once, so the button is used to cycle through three different views. We're using PyBBIO here because it includes a library to control character LCDs:

```
from bbio import *
from bbio.libraries.LiquidCrystal import LiquidCrystal
import psutil, threading

tmp36 = AIN4
```

```
button = GPIO0_20

RS_PIN = GPIO0_30
RW_PIN = GPIO0_31
EN_PIN = GPIO1_16
D4_PIN = GPIO0_5
D5_PIN = GPIO0_13
D6_PIN = GPIO0_3
D7_PIN = GPIO1_17
lcd = LiquidCrystal(RS_PIN, RW_PIN, EN_PIN, D4_PIN, D5_PIN,
  D6_PIN, D7_PIN)

screen = 0

def get_external_temp_c():
    v = inVolts(analogRead(tmp36))
    return (v - 0.75) * 100.0 + 25

def get_cpu_temp_c():
        with open('/sys/class/hwmon/hwmon0/device/temp1_input',
            'r') as f:return int(f.read()) / 1000

def poll_button():
    while True:
        global screen
        if (digitalRead(button) == LOW):
            screen = (screen+1) % 3
            while(digitalRead(button) == LOW): delay(10)
        delay(50)

def setup():
    lcd.begin(16, 2) # (columns, rows)
    pinMode(button, INPUT, PULLUP)
    t = threading.Thread(target=poll_button)
    t.daemon = True
    t.start()

def loop():
    if (screen == 0):
        line1 = "Ext temp : {}C".format(get_external_temp_c())
        line2 = "CPU temp : {}C".format(get_cpu_temp_c())
    elif (screen == 1):
        line1 = "CPU : {}%".format(psutil.cpu_percent())
        line2 = "Mem : {}%".format(psutil.virtual_memory()[2])
```

```
else:
    net_info = psutil.net_io_counters()
    line1 = "eth0  up : {}".format(net_info[2])
    line2 = "eth0 dwn : {}".format(net_info[3])
lcd.clear()
lcd.home()
lcd.prints(line1)
lcd.goto(0, 1) # go to column 0, row 1
lcd.prints(line2)
delay(500)

run(setup, loop)
```

Note how the button input is being received. It is utilizing the method described in *Chapter 5*, *User Input*, in which the button is ignored until it is released, but it does so in a separate thread in order to avoid interfering with the LCD drawing. This could be done in the same thread without blocking the LCD drawing by using global flags to track the state of the button, but we might as well take advantage of the parallelization tools Python provides to keep the code straightforward.

Summary

In this chapter, you learned a number of ways to provide output to the user from your BeagleBone programs. You learned how to interface with and control different types of LED and LCD displays, as well as how to have your BeagleBone send messages to you remotely. You built an unread e-mail notification system, a thermometer, a motion detection system, and two different system resource monitors for your BeagleBone Black.

In the next chapter, you will learn how the I2C and SPI protocols work, and how to use them with Python.

7

Serial Communication

In this chapter, you will learn how to use the BeagleBone's serial communication subsystems. We will cover the following topics:

- UART
- I2C
- SPI

Serial communication

Serial communication is the process of sending data a single bit at a time, or serially. Alternatively, in parallel communication, the data is sent in sets of simultaneous bits each on separate wires. Serial communication came about largely because of the cost of parallel cables, as each parallel bit would have to have its own wire. It's especially more cost efficient in the case where you are transferring data over long distances. There tends to be more complexity involved in parallel communication, and as factors, such as processor speeds have increased over the years, thus increasing the speed at which data can be serialized, serial communication has become much more widely used. Serial buses are now the primary way for devices to communicate with each other between different systems, as well as locally on the same circuit board.

UART

A UART is one of the most common serial communication subsystems. To transmit data with a UART, one or more bytes are written to an internal shift register by a CPU from where they are then serially sent out; a single output is sent out at a previously defined clock rate. Another UART (programmed to run at the same clock rate as the first), with its single input connected to the output of the first, detects the start of this bit stream, and it sequentially reads the bits into its own internal shift register. Once all the bits are sent, the receiving UART signals its CPU to let it know there's data ready, and the CPU then reads it out of the receive register.

A UARTs transmit output is referred to as TX, and its received input as RX. They often have some additional signals for more advanced handshaking, called flow control, which help ensure synchronization. We'll only cover the RX and TX signals here, as we won't be using the flow control signals in any of the demos in this book. Synchronization between two UARTs is typically achieved without the additional flow control signals by prepending one or more start bits to each byte to mark its start, and sometimes one or more stop bits are appended to each byte to mark its end. Two UARTs are connected together by wiring the TX signal from one to the RX input of the other, and vice versa.

Communication between two UARTs completely relies on them running at the same speed, as they must agree on how much time the digital state is held for each bit. The measurement of speed used for UARTs is the baud rate, or symbols per second, where a symbol refers to what encodes a single bit. In more advanced communication protocols, there can be more than one pulse per bit to provide error immunity, but in a standard UART communication there is one pulse per bit, so the baud rate is equivalent to the rate in bits per second.

There are a number of standard baud rates used: 110, 300, 600, 1200, 2400, 4800, 9600, 14400, 19200, 28800, 38400, 56000, 57600, and 115200 symbols/second. Many modern UARTs also support the higher standard rates of 128000, 153600, 230400, 256000, 460800, and 921600 symbols/second. Some UARTs can autodetect the baud rate of a device connected to it, but typically both endpoints will have been programmed ahead of time to use the same baud.

The BeagleBone's processor contains six separate UART modules, labeled UART0 - UART5. UART0 is reserved for a serial console, as described in *Chapter 2, Getting Started*, and UART3 is not fully exposed on the expansion headers. That leaves UART1, UART2, UART4, and UART5 open for general use. These use the following pins on the expansion headers:

- UART1:
    ◦ RX - P9.26
    ◦ TX - P9.24

- UART2:
    ◦ RX - P9.22
    ◦ TX - P9.21

- UART4:
    - RX - P9.11
    - TX - P9.13

- UART5:
    - RX - P8.38
    - TX - P8.37

 The UART5 RX and TX signals are shared with pins used by the HDMI driver, so to use it HDMI must first be disabled. See *Appendix A, The BeagleBone Black Pinout*.

Each UART on the BeagleBone is enabled separately. As with the other subsystems, PyBBIO automatically loads the overlays to enable each UART when you initialize it. Otherwise, you'll have to enable them manually with capemgr by loading the overlays named BB-UART1, BB-UART2, BB-UART4, and BB-UART5. When the overlay is loaded, a device node will be created, which is a special kernel driver interface file in /dev/ directory. The BeagleBone's kernel calls these device nodes /dev/ttyOx, where x is the UART number. So enabling UART2 with the BB-UART2 overlay will create the device node at /dev/ttyO2 (note that's the letter O following tty, not the number 0). Inside the operating system abstraction, these particular virtual devices are referred to as serial ports. The serial port kernel driver allows you to control a UART by writing to and reading from its device node as if it were a regular file, with some initial setup with ioctl to configure parameters like the baud rate.

 ioctl is a system call on Unix-like systems that takes three arguments:

- A file descriptor of an open special file, such as a device node for a serial port
- A request code (specific to the device driver in question) describing what parameter you want to read or manipulate
- An address in memory where a read parameter will be placed, or where a value is stored if you're making a change

ioctlis used to read and manipulate parameters that don't fit into the standard file read/write m

In PyBBIO, there is a preinstantiated object for each UART, named Serial1, Serial2, Serial4, and Serial5 respectively. The full API docs can be found on the PyBBIO wiki page at `https://github.com/graycatlabs/PyBBIO/wiki/serial`. As an example, here's a simple program that listens for incoming data on UART2, receives it, and then transmits it back out from UART2:

```
from bbio import *

def setup():
    # Start Serial2 at 9600 baud:
    Serial2.begin(9600)

def loop():
    if (Serial2.available()):
        # There's incoming data
        data = ""
        while(Serial2.available()):
            # If multiple characters are being sent we want
            # to catch them all, so add received byte to our
            # data string and delay a little to give the
            # next byte time to arrive:
            data += Serial2.read()
            delay(5)
        # Print what was sent:
        print "Data received:\n '%s'" % data
        # And echo it back to the serial port:
        Serial2.write(data)
    delay(100)

run(setup, loop)
```

You can test this program with the USB to serial converter from Adafruit (`http://www.adafruit.com/products/70`) mentioned in *Chapter 2*, *Getting Started*; hook up the black ground wire to a GND pin (like P9.1), the orange TX wire to the UART2 RX pin (P9.22), and the yellow RX wire to the UART2 TX pin (P9.21), as shown (where the arrows indicate the direction of data flow):

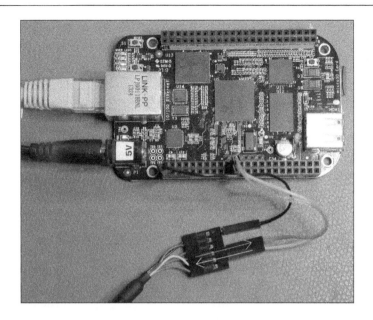

You'll need to first install the driver for the USB to the serial converter inside the cable, which you can find at `http://www.ftdichip.com/Drivers/VCP.htm`. With the driver installed, when you plug the serial cable into a Windows PC, it should detect it and assign it a COM port number. If you're not sure what number it was assigned, you can check for a **USB Serial Port(COM15)** entry in **Device Manager**:

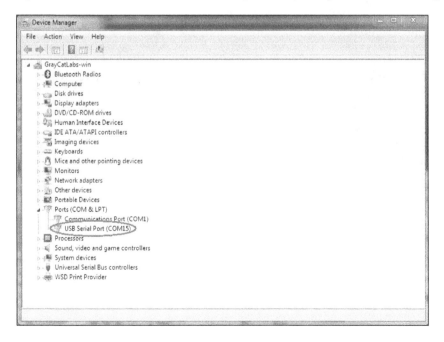

In the screenshot, you can see it was assigned **COM15**. Now open PuTTY (which we used previously in *Chapter 2, Getting Started*), select **Serial line** and enter the COM port and baud rate:

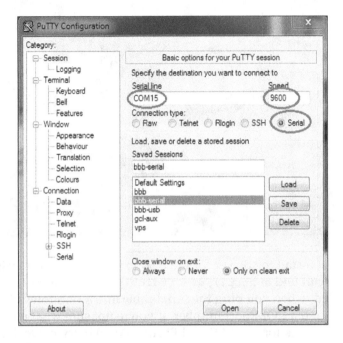

We've used the 9600 baud rate here, since that's what we're using in the example program; any standard baud rate will work as long as they're both the same.

Get the example program running on your BeagleBone Black and then press **Open** in PuTTY. You'll be dropped into a terminal window where you can type characters on your keyboard, which are sent to the converter IC in the USB cable, sent out to the ICs UART over the cable, and received in the BeagleBone Black's UART2. The characters are read by the Python program, printed to the terminal where it's running, then they are sent back through the serial cable to your PC where they are received and displayed on the PuTTY terminal. We can see this happening with an oscilloscope:

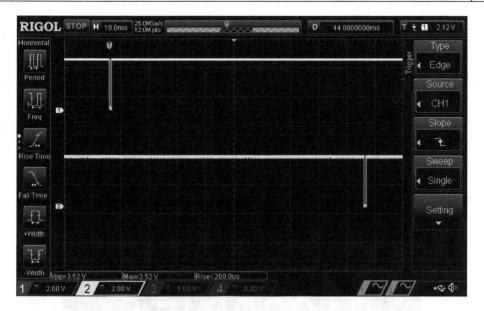

In the oscilloscope screenshot, the yellow trace shows voltage from a probe connected to the PC's TX signal going to the BeagleBone's RX pin, and the blue trace shows the signal from the BeagleBone's TX pin being sent to the PC. We can see that there is data being sent from the PC to the BeagleBone, then a short time later, there is data being sent back to the PC. Let's zoom in a little closer on the first chunk of data:

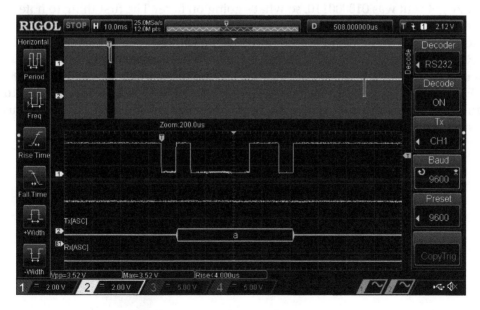

Here, you can see that the serial decode feature has been enabled on the oscilloscope, and it shows us that the data sent is the ASCII character "a". In ASCII, the letter "a" is encoded as 0x61, or in binary, 01100001.

 You might also notice that the decoder selected on the oscilloscope screenshot is called **RS232**. **RS232** is a serial transmission standard. PCs used to always include serial ports to connect peripheral devices such as modems and printers, and is still widely used in commercial and industrial applications. While the voltage levels we're using here are different from RS232, standard UARTs still use the same basic serializing protocol.

Let's take a closer look at the byte we recorded to make sure we agree with the decoder:

We just said that the binary value of the ASCII character "a" is 01100001, but what actually got sent was 010000110, so what's going on here? The first thing to note is that this is in fact 9 bits, which is one bit longer than a standard 8-bit byte. The reason for this is that the first bit sent is actually a start bit, which tells the receiving UART that a byte is on the way. So that leaves 10000110, which is the binary value of a in reverse. That's because the data is being serialized in the **Least Significant Bit First (LSB)** order, where the byte is transmitted right-to-left, as opposed to **Most Significant Bit First (MSB)**, where the byte would be transmitted left-to-right; this is the standard bit ordering used by UARTs.

And if we zoom in to the byte that the BeagleBone sends back, we can see that it is also the ASCII character **a**:

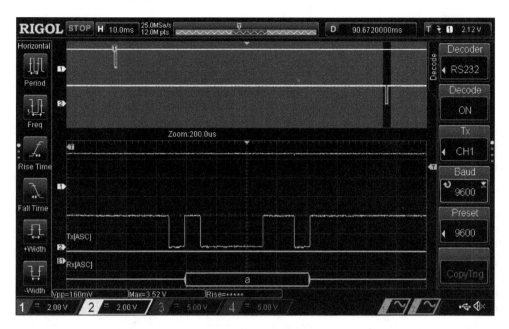

Adafruit_BBIO doesn't include its own objects for controlling the serial ports, but the pySerial Python library, which PyBBIO's serial port class is built on top, can be used directly in an Adafruit_BBIO program. The pySerial API can be found at http://pyserial.sourceforge.net/pyserial_api.html. The equivalent echo program using pySerial would look like this:

```python
import serial, time

port = serial.Serial("/dev/ttyO2", 9600)

while True:
    if (port.inWaiting()):
        data = ""
        while(port.inWaiting()):
            data += port.read()
            time.sleep(0.005)
        # Print what was sent:
        print "Data received:\n '%s'" % data
        port.write(data)
    time.sleep(0.1)
```

Remember, if you're not using PyBBIO, you'll need to manually load the Device Tree overlay to enable the UART, for example:

```
# echo BB-UART2 > /sys/devices/bone_capemgr.*/slots
```

I2C

In the I2C protocol, there's a master device controlling one or more slave devices using two digital signals. One of the signals is a clock, called **Serial Clock (SCL)**, and the other is a bidirectional data line, called **Serial Data (SDA)**. The clock signal is generated by the master, which means the devices don't need to be programmed with the same symbol rate like UARTs do.

To handle multiple devices, each slave device on the same bus (sharing the same SDA and SCL signals) must have an individual address. The standard I2C protocol uses 7-bit slave addresses, meaning there can be up to $2^7 = 128$ devices on a single bus. There are 16 addresses reserved for special purposes, so that leaves room for 112 general I2C devices per bus. A device's address is programmed into it by its manufacturer, and there is no guarantee that any two devices won't have the same address, so in practice, the upper limit would likely be less than 112. Some devices have a single hardcoded address and some devices can be set to one of a few hardcoded addresses by pulling external address pins high or low.

When the I2C master wants to communicate with a slave device, it must first send a header, which includes the address of the device it wants to communicate with, as well as a bit, called the R/W bit, which tells the slave if the master is intending to write data to it or read data from it. To send these bits, the master pulls the clock line low, sets the data line according to the current bit value, sets the clock line high, and then repeats for each subsequent bit. The slave device reads the state of the data line when it detects the rising edge of the clock line. Once the address and R/W bit have been sent, the master sets its data pin to an input state and the slave device sets its data pin to an output state. When the slave device detects the next falling clock edge from the master, it sets the data line high to indicate it has acknowledged the packet, or sets it low to indicate that it has not acknowledged it. This is referred to as an ACK or NACK, respectively. If the R/W bit is 1, meaning that the master will be writing to the device, the data line once again is controlled by the master and the data is written one byte at a time, with each byte concluding with the ACK/NACK bit from the slave. If the R/W bit is 0 to indicate read mode, the slave remains in control of the data line, shifting bits out as the master toggles the clock line.

There are a few clock rates defined for I2C buses—100 kilobit/s standard speed, 400 kilobit/s full speed, 1 megabit/s fast mode, and 3.2 megabit/s high speed. The BeagleBone I2C buses all operate at the 100 kilobit/s standard speed.

The BeagleBone Black has two I2C buses available on its expansion headers:

- I2C1
  - ° SCL - P9.17
  - ° SDA - P9.18

- I2C2
  - ° SCL - P9.19
  - ° SDA - P9.20

There is an additional I2C0 bus on the BeagleBone Black, but it is used for communication between onboard ICs and is not accessible on the expansion headers.

The three I2C buses are controlled through the `/dev/i2c-0`, `/dev/i2c-1`, and `/dev/i2c-1` device nodes. The BeagleBone Black's kernel numbers the I2C buses in the order in which they appear, and these numbers don't correspond to the actual bus numbers. However, I2C0 and I2C2 are both enabled by default (I2C2 is used to detect expansion capes), and are therefore controlled through `/dev/i2c-0` and `/dev/i2c-1`, respectively. I2C1 can be enabled by loading the BB-I2C1 Device Tree overlay, which creates the next device node `/dev/i2c-2`. So to summarize, `/dev/i2c-0` controls I2C0 (used internally and should be left alone), `/dev/i2c-1` controls I2C2, and `/dev/i2c-2` controls I2C1 (when enabled with `capemgr`). When using PyBBIO, the I2C1 overlay is loaded automatically if it is being used, and you don't need to worry about the device node numbering. With Adafuit_BBIO, you will have to remember the numbering scheme because the port being used is specified by the device node numbering.

Let's look at an example of using an I2C bus by hooking up a Melexis MLX90614 contactless IR temperature sensor (`http://www.adafruit.com/products/1747`) to the I2C2 bus.

 The MLX90614 is a fairly pricey sensor, and we won't go very deep into software for it, so there's no real need to follow along. If you are building the circuit up for yourself, though, make sure to use the 3 V version of the sensor and not the 5 V version; otherwise, you could damage the sensor and/or your BeagleBone.

The circuit is pretty simple:

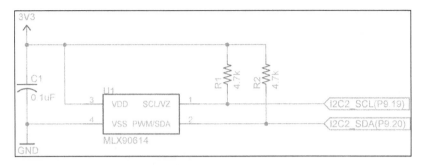

As you can see, there are two pull-up resistors on the SCL and SDA lines. These are a requirement of the I2C protocol, and it won't function without them. The pull-up on the SDA line ensures that it will be at a high level during the transition between master and slave control, and the pull-up on the SCL line will ensure that there are no false clock pulses if the master device gets reset.

There is also a suite of command line tools to help with using I2C from user-space on GNU/Linux called `i2c-tools`, which you can install from `apt-get` on Debian:

```
# apt-get install i2c-tools
```

One of these tools is `i2cdetect`, which is able to probe I2C buses for slave devices. With the MLX90614 hooked up to I2C2, we can run the tool and find its address:

```
root@beaglebone:~# i2cdetect -r 1
WARNING! This program can confuse your I2C bus, cause data loss and
worse!
I will probe file /dev/i2c-1 using read byte commands.
I will probe address range 0x03-0x77.
Continue? [Y/n] y
     0  1  2  3  4  5  6  7  8  9  a  b  c  d  e  f
00:          -- -- -- -- -- -- -- -- -- -- -- -- --
10: -- -- -- -- -- -- -- -- -- -- -- -- -- -- -- --
20: -- -- -- -- -- -- -- -- -- -- -- -- -- -- -- --
30: -- -- -- -- -- -- -- -- -- -- -- -- -- -- -- --
40: -- -- -- -- -- -- -- -- -- -- -- -- -- -- -- --
50: -- -- -- -- UU UU UU UU -- -- 5a -- -- -- -- --
60: -- -- -- -- -- -- -- -- -- -- -- -- -- -- -- --
70: -- -- -- -- -- -- -- --
```

This table tells us that the MLX90614 has an address of 0x5a (which we can also find in the datasheet), and is connected and responding properly. The datasheet tells us that we can read the temperature of the object the sensor is pointing at by first writing the command `0x07` to it, then by reading the three bytes. We can also read the ambient temperature inside the sensor the same way, but instead using the `0x06` command.

PyBBIO provides two objects, I2C1 and I2C2, for controlling the I2C buses. The full I2C API can be found on the PyBBIO wiki page at `https://github.com/graycatlabs/PyBBIO/wiki/I2C`. It is common for I2C devices to use the protocol of writing a byte before reading, so that it knows what to send (which can correspond to a command, as with the MLX90614, or it can be the address of a register in the slave device's memory, which you want to access); so along with the individual `read()` and `write()` methods, PyBBIO also provides a method called `readTransaction()`, which does just that. So to read the temperature from the device we will first enable the bus:

```
root@beaglebone:~# python
Python 2.7.3 (default, Mar 14 2014, 17:55:54)
[GCC 4.6.3] on linux2
Type "help", "copyright", "credits" or "license" for more information.
>>> from bbio import *
PyBBIO initialized
>>> I2C2.open()
```

Then, we will call `readTransaction()`, giving it the address of the MLX90614, the `0x07` command byte to write, and the number of bytes to read:

```
>>> I2C2.readTransaction(0x5a, 0x07, 3)
[41, 58, 179]
```

The first two bytes received are the low and high bytes of the measured temperature, respectively. The third byte received is an 8-bit cyclic redundancy check (CRC-8) calculated from the temperature data, which can be used to detect whether the data was corrupted due to transmission errors.

Let's take a look at the SDA and SCL signals when we read the temperature:

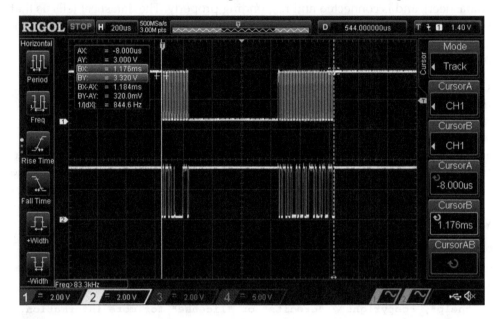

The top trace in the capture is the SCL signal and the bottom is SDA. You can distinctly see the separate write and read sections of the transaction. Let's take a closer look at the first section:

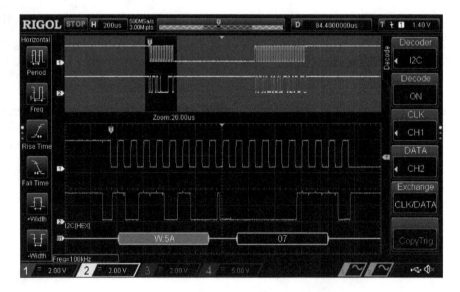

The first thing sent is the address, with the R/W bit set to write, followed by the 0x07 command. Also notice that the bytes are being sent in the MSB first order, as opposed to the LSB first order that the UARTs use. Now we'll zoom in on the second section:

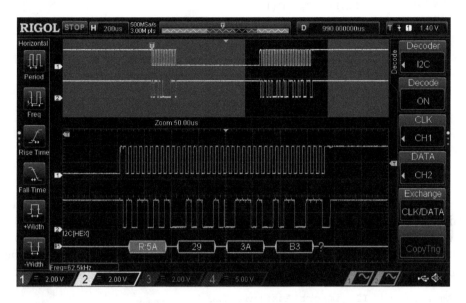

The second part of the transaction is started with another header, but this time with the R/W bit set to read, then the three data bytes are received. As soon as the header is sent, the MLX90614 takes control of the SDA line.

For the sake of completeness, here's a small program to show you how the two temperatures can be read and converted from the MLX90614 using PyBBIO:

```python
from bbio import *

def readObjectTempC():
    low, high, pec = I2C2.readTransaction(0x5a, 0x07, 3)
    tempk = ((high << 8) | low)*0.02 # temp in Kelvin
    return tempk - 273.75 # Convert to Celsius

def readAmbientTempC():
    low, high, pec  = I2C2.readTransaction(0x5a, 0x06, 3)
    tempk = ((high << 8) | low)*0.02
    return tempk - 273.75

def setup():
    I2C2.open()
```

```
def loop():
    print "ambient = {:0.2f} C - object = {:0.2f} C".format(
          readAmbientTempC(),
          readObjectTempC()
          )
    delay(500)

run(setup, loop)
```

`Adafruit_BBIO` provides the `Adafruit_I2C` class, which is fully documented at https://learn.adafruit.com/setting-up-io-python-library-on-beaglebone-black/i2c. You'll first need to install the `python-smbus` package that it depends on:

 # apt-get install python-smbus

`Adafruit_BBIO` uses a slightly different abstraction than PyBBIO for I2C, where the Adafruit_I2C object is instantiated with the address of a remote device. In other words, there is one Adafruit_I2C instance per slave device, as opposed to PyBBIO's I2C1 and I2C2 objects, which each represent an entire I2C bus. Reading the temperature from the MLX90614 with `Adafruit_BBIO` would look like this:

```
from Adafruit_I2C import Adafruit_I2C
i2c = Adafruit_I2C(0x5a, 1) # bus 1 for /dev/i2c-1, or I2C2
data = i2c.readList(0x07, 3)
```

SPI

SPI is, in its most typical form, a 4-wire protocol. Like I2C, it is a single-master, multiple-slave protocol. It has a clock line (SCK), a data line from the master to the slaves (MOSI), a data line from the slaves to the master (MISO), and a separate chip select (CS) line for each slave device. The CS signal for a particular slave device is pulled low by the master before communicating with it, and any other device on the same bus with its CS line set high will ignore any transferred data. SPI requires more pins than I2C, but unlike I2C it doesn't require transactions to include a slave address header, and it has separate data lines for each direction of communication (which can transfer data simultaneously). For these reasons, it can typically achieve higher data rates than I2C. The number of devices that can be put on the same SPI bus is dictated by the number of available pins for CS signals.

The SPI protocol is less strictly defined than I2C, with the bit order, clock mode, and clock speed all being configurable. The clock mode is made up of two bits, the clock polarity (CPOL) bit and the clock phase (CPHA) bit. These bits are as follows:

- **CPOL=0**: SCK is idle low (low level when no data is being sent)
  - ° **CPHA=0**: Data bits are set on the SCK falling edge and read on the SCK rising edge
  - ° **CPHA=1**: Data bits are set on the SCK rising edge and read on the SCK falling edge

- **CPOL=1**: SCK is idle high
  - ° **CPHA=0**: Data bits are set on the SCK rising edge and read on the SCK falling edge
  - ° **CPHA=1**: Data bits are set on the SCK falling edge and read on the SCK rising edge

A particular SPI device will specify the clock settings it uses, and it's up to the master device to ensure that it sets the clock mode accordingly. An SPI master can communicate with slave devices that have different clock modes on the same bus by simply changing the clock mode between interactions with each device.

There are no real standard SPI clock speeds, and SPI devices typically specify their maximum supported clock frequency. The device with the slowest maximum frequency on an SPI bus dictates the maximum bus speed.

The BeagleBone Black has two SPI ports available on its expansion headers, SPI0 and SPI1, with the pins:

- **SPI0**:
  - ° CS0 - P9_17
  - ° MISO - P9_21
  - ° MOSI - P9_18
  - ° SCLK - P9_22

- **SPI1**:
  - ° CS0 - P9_28
  - ° CS1 - P9_42
  - ° MISO - P9_29
  - ° MOSI - P9_30
  - ° SCLK - P9_31

You'll have to disable HDMI to use SPI1, as described in *Appendix B, Disabling HDMI.*

The SPI modules are enabled by loading Device Tree overlays with `capemgr`, called BB-SPIDEV0 and BB-SPIDEV1. These create the device nodes `/dev/spidev1.0`, `/dev/spidev1.1`, `/dev/spidev2.0`, and `/dev/spidev2.1`. The first number in each device name corresponds to an SPI bus, while the second number corresponds to a CS signal. As for I2C, the bus number in the device nodes is assigned according to the order in which the buses are enabled. Neither SPI bus is enabled by default, so you'll have to keep track of the order in which you enable them. Again, if you're using PyBBIO, this is kept track of behind the scenes for you.

Since SPI0 only has its CS0 signal exposed on the headers, and not its CS1 signal, the `/dev/spidevX.1` device node corresponding to SPI0 will not control any external CS signal on the expansion headers. If you need more than two devices connected to one of the SPI buses, you can simply use GPIO pins for chip select signals instead.

In PyBBIO, initializing an SPI bus is similar to I2C or UART:

```
root@beaglebone:~# python
Python 2.7.3 (default, Mar 14 2014, 17:55:54)
[GCC 4.6.3] on linux2
Type "help", "copyright", "credits" or "license" for more information.
>>> from bbio import *
PyBBIO initialized
>>> SPI0.open()
```

It's also good to set your clock frequency to a known value to make sure you're not running faster than any of the connected devices support, for example 1 MHz:

```
>>> SPI0.setMaxFrequency(0,1000000)
```

To then write out a byte of data, would be as follows:

```
>>> SPI0.write(0, [0x61])
```

Where the first number is the CS signal to use and the second is a list of bytes to be sent sequentially. We can see this transmission in action on the oscilloscope:

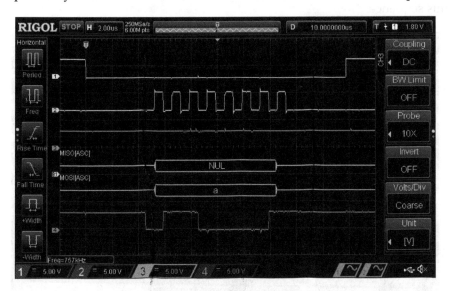

The top yellow trace is the CS signal, which you can see being pulled low at the start of the transmission and driven high at the end. The light blue trace below it is the clock signal. The default clock mode for the BeagleBone Black's SPI modules is CPOL = 0 and CPHA = 0, so the clock is idle and low and the data is read on the rising edge (the clock mode can be configured with the setClockMode() method). The clock signal has eight rising edges for the eight bits in the byte we sent. The pink trace is the MISO line, the data being received by the master, and it is unchanged since there's no data being received. The dark blue trace at the bottom shows the bits sent on the MOSI line, and the SPI decoder shows that it is the ASCII character "a" as expected.

As a quick test to make sure we are receiving data as expected, we can simply connect the MOSI and MISO signals to create a data loopback. If we do this and send a few more bytes, as follows:

```
>>> SPI0.transfer(0, [0x61, 0x62, 0x63])
[97, 98, 99]
```

Then, we can see that the data with the same bytes is received (which are integers, so Python prints them as decimal values). Let's take a look at the oscilloscope when we send this sequence:

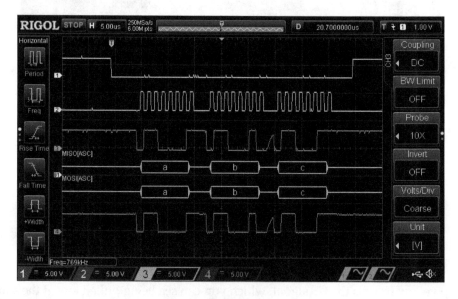

As you can see, the same data is now present on the MISO line because we connected it to MOSI. We can also see that the CS line is held low for the entire transmission instead of toggled between bytes.

As mentioned previously, to use SPI from `Adafruit_BBIO`, you'll need to first load the BB-SPIDEV0 or BB-SPIDEV1 Device Tree overlay. You'll then need to take note of the bus number assigned to the `spidev` device node entry that was created. If you're only using one SPI bus, this will be 1 for `/dev/spidev1.x`. You then need to create an instance of the `Adafruit_BBIO.SPI` class for each bus and CS pin you are using. `Adafruit_BBIO` numbers the buses starting from 0, so to use SPI1 with CS0 it will be:

```
from Adafruit_BBIO.SPI import SPI
spi = SPI(0,0)
spi.writebytes([0x61])
```

The documentation for the `Adafruit_BBIO` SPI class can be found at `https://learn.adafruit.com/setting-up-io-python-library-on-beaglebone-black/spi`.

Summary

In this chapter, you learned the basics of the UART, I2C, and SPI modules and their serial protocols. We looked briefly at how these protocols are implemented on the BeagleBone Black and how to control them from Python.

In the next chapter, we will look at a more in-depth example of using the I2C protocol to interface with an external sensor.

8
Interfacing with External Devices

In this chapter, we will work through the process of interfacing with a new device. We will cover the following topics:

- Reading datasheets
- I2C sensor memory registers
- Accelerometer basics
- Accelerometer interrupt functions
- Writing Python libraries for external devices
- Tap detection as input

Accelerometers

Accelerometers, made abundant and affordable by the cell phone industry, are one of the most common sensors found in embedded devices these days. As their name implies, accelerometers sense acceleration, in one, two, or three axes. This is useful for things, such as pedometers, as you can sense the vibrations from a footstep, and they can also be used for sensing orientation by measuring the acceleration due to gravity on the different axes.

Hooking it up

Let's take a look at interfacing with the analog devices' ADXL345 accelerometer. It can measure acceleration about three axes on a configurable scale of +/- 2 g, 4 g, 8 g or 16 g (where 1 g is the acceleration due to gravity near the Earth's surface, equal to about 9.8 m/s²) about three axes. Both SparkFun and Adafruit sell breakout boards for the ADXL345 (`https://www.sparkfun.com/products/9836` and `http://www.adafruit.com/product/1231`). We'll demonstrate with the SparkFun board, but the Adafruit board will function just the same; just be sure to follow their wiring instructions. Both boards come with male header pins that you'll have to solder on yourself to use them with a breadboard.

For this circuit, you will need:

- Breadboard
- 1x ADXL345 breakout board
- 2x 4.7 kΩ resistors
- Jumper wires

Hook up the accelerometer as shown:

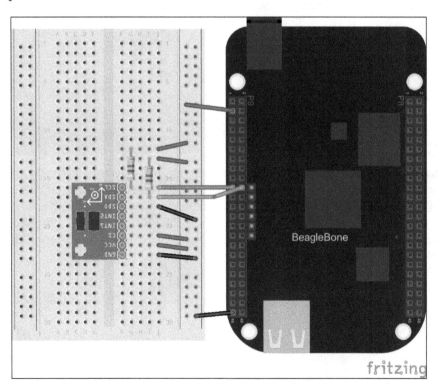

The ADXL345 is wired to the I2C2 bus, and the two 4.7 kΩ resistors are the pull-up resistors required by the I2C spec, as described in *Chapter 7, Serial Communication*. Make a note of the CS and SDO pins; the ADXL345 gives you the choice of an SPI or I2C interface, and, keeping the CS pin high, we tell it we are using I2C. The SDO pin is the data output when in the SPI mode, and in the I2C mode, it is used to choose between two different I2C addresses by pulling it high or low. The INT1 and INT2 pins are interrupt output signals, which can be configured to send an interrupt signal to the processor when different events are detected, such as shakes and free-falls. We're not using the interrupts here, so we can just leave them unconnected.

Reading data

When connecting a new device, the first thing you'll need is its datasheet, which describes its electrical and mechanical properties, and how to interface with it. The ADXL345 datasheet can be found on analog device's site at http://www.analog.com/media/en/technical-documentation/data-sheets/ADXL345.pdf.

The first thing we'll need from the datasheet is the I2C address. The I2C section of the datasheet tells us that its address is 0x1D when ALT ADDRESS (the SDO pin) is pulled high, and 0x53 when it is low. We've pulled it low in our wiring, so the address should be 0x53. We can confirm this once it's connected using the following i2cdetect tool:

```
root@beaglebone:~# i2cdetect -r 1
WARNING! This program can confuse your I2C bus, cause data loss and
worse!
I will probe file /dev/i2c-1 using read byte commands.
I will probe address range 0x03-0x77.
Continue? [Y/n] y
     0  1  2  3  4  5  6  7  8  9  a  b  c  d  e  f
00:          -- -- -- -- -- -- -- -- -- -- -- --
10: -- -- -- -- -- -- -- -- -- -- -- -- -- -- -- --
20: -- -- -- -- -- -- -- -- -- -- -- -- -- -- -- --
30: -- -- -- -- -- -- -- -- -- -- -- -- -- -- -- --
40: -- -- -- -- -- -- -- -- -- -- -- -- -- -- -- --
50: -- -- -- 53 UU UU UU UU -- -- -- -- -- -- -- --
60: -- -- -- -- -- -- -- -- -- -- -- -- -- -- -- --
70: -- -- -- -- -- -- -- --
```

This table shows us that there is in fact a device connected at the address 0x53.

Now, let's jump to the register map, which you can find in the datasheet's index. The ADXL345 works similarly to many sensors and other I2C devices, where the processor controls it by reading from and writing to its memory registers directly. This table shows us the address of each memory register we have access to, whether or not they can be written to or read, and irrespective of what their reset value is.

The register at memory location 0x00 is a read only device ID, which should have the binary value 11100101. This gives us an easy way to double check that everything is hooked up correctly and working. Hop into a bash shell by opening a new terminal in Cloud9 or by SSHing into your BeagleBone, and start the Python interactive interpreter. We'll use PyBBIO to read the device ID register:

```
# python
>>> from bbio import *
>>> Wire2.open()
>>> bin(Wire2.readTransaction(0x53, 0x0, 1)[0])
'0b11100101'
```

Now that we know we are connected correctly and talking to the accelerometer, we can proceed with getting it set up.

The only thing we actually need to change to start the ADXL345 sampling is the Measure bit in the POWER_CTL register (0x2D). Setting this bit to 1 puts the ADXL345 into the full power sampling mode. It also supports various low power modes, but we don't really care about power consumption here, so we won't worry about that. Measure is bit 3, where the least significant bit is bit 0 and they go up to the left, so its value when set is 1<<3. We want to leave the rest of the bits in this register set to 0 for normal operation:

```
>>> Wire2.write(0x53, [0x2D, 1<<3])
```

Your ADXL345 should now be sampling three axes of acceleration data at its default rate of 100Hz, with its default range of +/- 2 g. With the sensor on a breadboard and the breadboard flat on your table or workbench, the Z-axis should be roughly parallel to the Earth's gravitational pull, so we'll read a sample from the Z-axis to see if we can detect the effect.

The Z-axis data is stored as a 16-bit number in registers 0x36 and 0x37, where 0x36 holds the least significant byte and 0x37 the most significant byte. So we'll first need to get the raw values from the sensor:

```
>>> data = Wire2.readTransaction(0x53, 0x36, 2)
```

Next, we'll need to combine them into one number by shifting the MSB 8 bits to the left and bitwise ORing them together:

```
>>> sample = (data[1] << 8) | data[0]
```

The value is stored in two's complement format to support negative numbers. In general, to convert a two's complement number of N bits to a signed value, if it is greater than or equal to 2^{N-1}, then you subtract 2^N from it. So for the 16-bit number, here, we use 2^{15} and 2^{16}. Let's have a look at the following command:

```
>>> if sample >= 2**15: sample -= 2**16
```

And finally, we want it in units of g. To do this, we first need to calculate the value in g of a 1. The sensor's default resolution is 10-bits, so a 1 would be the full span of the current range, which is 4g for the default +/- 2g , divided by the resolution of 2^{10} bits. So that's *4 g/2^{10} bits = 0.00390625 g/bit*. Now multiply the sample by this value and you'll have a value in g, which should be right around 1 g:

```
>>> sample*0.00390625
0.96875
```

Writing a module

If we want to write programs that use the ADXL345, it will be helpful to have a nice API for it. The object-oriented programming paradigm lends itself well to abstracting hardware devices, so let's define a simple class for the accelerometer that we can use in other programs:

```
class ADXL345(object):
  def __init__(self, i2c):
    self.i2c = i2c

  def begin(self):
    self.i2c.open()
    self.i2c.write(0x53, [0x2D, 1<<3])

  def get_xyz(self):
    data = self.i2c.readTransaction(0x53, 0x32, 6)
    samples = [0]*3
    for i in range(3):
      samples[i] = (data[i+i+1]<<8) | data[i+i]
      if samples[i] >= 32768: samples[i] -= 65536
      samples[i] *= 0.00390625
      return samples
```

If you save that to a file called `adxl345.py`, you can then import it into another file in the same directory to test it out:

```
from bbio import *
from adxl345 import ADXL345

accel = ADXL345(Wire2)

def setup():
  accel.begin()

def loop():
  x, y, z = accel.get_xyz()
  print "X: {:0.2f}g, Y: {:0.2f}g, Z: {:0.2f}g".format(x,y,z)
  delay(200)


run(setup, loop)
```

If you give the breadboard a shake, you'll notice that it doesn't take much to make it max out the +/- 2 g range. So let's add a method to set the range. Back in the register definitions, we can see that bits B0 and B1 of the DATA_FORMAT register (0x31) set the range, where 0-3 correspond to +/-2 g, 4 g, 8 g, and 16 g. The reset value of all the bits in the DATA_FORMAT register is 0, so we can leave the rest as is and only set the two range bits. Add this new method to your ADXL345 class:

```
class ADXL345(object):
  RANGE_2G  = 0
  RANGE_4G  = 1
  RANGE_8G  = 2
  RANGE_16G = 3
  # Pre-calculated unit conversion multipliers:
  G_PER_BIT = [
    0.00390625,
    0.0078125,
    0.015625,
    0.03125
  ]

  def __init__(self, i2c, addr=0x53):
    self.i2c = i2c
    self.addr = addr

  def begin(self):
    self.i2c.open()
    self.i2c.write(0x53, [0x2D, 1<<3])
```

```
    self.set_range(self.RANGE_2G)

  def get_xyz(self):
    data = self.i2c.readTransaction(0x53, 0x32, 6)
    samples = [0]*3
    for i in range(3):
      samples[i] = (data[i+i+1]<<8) | data[i+i]
      if samples[i] >= 32768: samples[i] -= 65536
      samples[i] *= self.G_PER_BIT[self.accel_range]
      return samples

  def set_range(self, accel_range):
    accel_range &= 0b11 # ensure it's only 2 bits
    self.i2c.write(self.addr, [0x31, accel_range])
    self.accel_range = accel_range
```

With the ability to change ranges, we also need to keep track of which range the ASXL345 is in for converting the values to g, and here we've also created a list of precalculated g/bit conversion multipliers. Since this class is becoming more useful, we've also made the I2C address an optional parameter so that it can support the alternative 0x1D address.

Now you can set the range in the test program, and you should start to see values greater than +/- 2g when you give it a good shake:

```
from bbio import *
from adxl345 import ADXL345

accel = ADXL345(Wire2)

def setup():
  accel.begin()
  accel.set_range(accel.RANGE_8G)

def loop():
  x, y, z = accel.get_xyz()
  print "X: {:0.2f}g, Y: {:0.2f}g, Z: {:0.2f}g".format(x,y,z)
  delay(200)

run(setup, loop)
```

Using interrupts

It's common for accelerometer ICs to support various interrupt functions along with reporting raw data. The ADXL345 class supports single and double tap detection, general activity and inactivity, and free-fall events. Any of these interrupts can be enabled simultaneously and can be routed to either of the two INT output pins.

Let's expand our ADXL345 class to support the tap detection interrupts. First we'll need a method to enable the interrupts and map them to the output pins. They are enabled through the INT_ENABLE register (0x2E), and mapped to the outputs in the INT_MAP register (0x2F). In both registers, bits 6 and 5 correspond to single tap and double tap, respectively, and a value of 1 in either bit maps the corresponding tap interrupt to the INT2 pin, while a 0 value maps it to the INT1 pin. So we can add a method to the ADXL345 class that takes an interrupt value of either 1<<6 (bit 6 set, for single tap) or 1<<5 (bit 5 set, for double tap), as well as an int_pin value of either 1 or 2 for INT1 or INT2, respectively:

```
INT_DOUBLE_TAP = 1<<5
INT_SINGLE_TAP = 1<<6
INT1 = 1
INT2 = 2

def enable_interrupt(self, interrupt, int_pin):
  # Map the interrupt to the pin:
  int_map = self.i2c.readTransaction(self.addr, 0x2F, 1)[0]
  if (int_pin == self.INT2):
    # bit=1 for INT2, set bit:
    int_map |= interrupt
  else:
    # bit=0 for INT1, clear bit:
    int_map &= ~interrupt
  self.i2c.write(self.addr, [0x2F, int_map])

  # Enable the interrupt
  int_enable = self.i2c.readTransaction(self.addr, 0x2E, 1)[0]
  int_enable |= interrupt # 1 to enable interrupt
  self.i2c.write(self.addr, [0x2E, int_enable])
```

So, for example, to enable INT1 and map it to the single tap interrupt signal, you would call accel.enable_interrupt(accel.INT_SINGLE_TAP, accel.INT1). This time we need to preserve the other bits in these registers to avoid disrupting the current interrupt configuration, so it's necessary to read the registers first, and set and clear only the desired bit in that value. That way you're writing the value currently in the register back to it with only the one bit changed. Now we know how to enable the interrupts, but we'll need to setup the tap detection before doing so.

A tap is detected by comparing the acceleration to a configured threshold in the THRESH_TAP register (0x1D). This register defaults to 0, so we'll need a method to change it so it's not constantly detecting taps once enabled. The datasheet tells us that the value in the threshold register is 16 g full-scale, so that makes the resolution $16\ g/2^8 = 0.0625\ g/bit$. To convert from g to bits, it will be X g / 0.0625 g/bit. Using this formula, our new method can take a threshold value in g and write the appropriate converted value to the register:

```
def set_tap_threshold(self, threshold):
  # Convert to bits:
  threshold /= 0.0625
  # Round to nearest integer:
  threshold = int(threshold + 0.5) # round to integer
  # Constrain to single byte:
  if threshold > 255: threshold = 255
  self.i2c.write(self.addr, [0x1D, threshold])
```

For a tap event to occur, the acceleration on any enabled axis must be above the value in THRESH_TAP for at least the time value set in the DUR register (0x21). Its default value of 0 means tap detection is disabled, so we'll need a method to set that as well. The DUR register scale is 625 µs/bit. At that scale, it's convenient to set the value in milliseconds, so to convert to bits, it would be X ms / 0.625 ms/bit. Add this method to set the duration value in milliseconds:

```
def set_tap_duration(self, duration):
  duration /= 0.625
  duration = int(duration + 0.5)
  if duration > 255: duration = 255
  self.i2c.write(self.addr, [0x21, duration])
```

A double tap event occurs if, and only if, a second tap is detected between Latent milliseconds and Window milliseconds, where Latent and Window are the values in the registers 0x22 and 0x23 respectively. In other words, Latent holds the minimum required delay between the two taps, and Window holds the maximum amount of time after Latent has expired in which the second tap can occur. Both of these registers must be set to a nonzero value for double tap detection to work, and both have a scale of 1.25 ms/bit. Let's add a new method for each:

```
def set_tap_latency(self, latency):
  latency /= 1.25
  latency = int(latency + 0.5)
  if latency > 255: latency = 255
  self.i2c.write(self.addr, [0x22, latency])

def set_tap_window(self, window):
  window /= 1.25
```

```
window = int(window + 0.5)
if window > 255: window = 255
self.i2c.write(self.addr, [0x23, window])
```

In addition to enabling the interrupts and configuring all the thresholds, each of the three axes has a tap detection enable bit in the TAP_AXES register (0x2A) that must be set. To keep things simple, we'll just enable tap detection on all axes. So we need one more method to enable the tap detection, and it might set some default configuration values as well:

```
def enable_tap_detection(self):
    # Enable taps for the different axes:
    self.i2c.write(self.addr, [0x2A, 0x7])
    self.set_tap_threshold(3) # 3g threshold
    self.set_tap_duration(20) # 20ms minimum duration
    self.set_tap_latency(100) # 100ms double-tap latency
    self.set_tap_window(1000) # 1s double-tap window
```

Finally, when a tap interrupt is detected, the interrupt status register has to be read to clear the pending interrupt before the next tap event can be detected. This simply means reading the INT_SOURCE register (0x30):

```
def get_interrupts(self):
    # Read and return INT_SOURCE register:
    return self.i2c.readTransaction(self.addr, 0x30, 1)[0]
```

So putting it all together, your class should look like this:

```
class ADXL345(object):
    RANGE_2G  = 0
    RANGE_4G  = 1
    RANGE_8G  = 2
    RANGE_16G = 3
    # Precalculated unit conversion multipliers:
    G_PER_BIT = [
        0.00390625,
        0.0078125,
        0.015625,
        0.03125
    ]
    INT_DOUBLE_TAP = 1<<5
    INT_SINGLE_TAP = 1<<6

    INT1 = 1
    INT2 = 2
```

```
def __init__(self, i2c, addr=0x53):
  self.i2c = i2c
  self.addr = addr

def begin(self):
  self.i2c.begin()
  self.i2c.write(self.addr, [0x2D, 1<<3])
  self.set_range(self.RANGE_2G)

def get_xyz(self):
  data = self.i2c.readTransaction(self.addr, 0x32, 6)
  samples = [0]*3
  for i in range(0, 3):
    samples[i] = (data[i+i+1]<<8) | data[i+i]
    if samples[i] >= 32768: samples[i] -= 65536
    samples[i] *= self.G_PER_BIT[self.accel_range]
    return samples

def set_range(self, accel_range):
  accel_range &= 0b11 # ensure it's only 2 bits
  self.i2c.write(self.addr, [0x31, accel_range])
  self.accel_range = accel_range

def enable_interrupt(self, interrupt, int_pin):
  # Map the interrupt to the pin:
  int_map = self.i2c.readTransaction(self.addr, 0x2F, 1)[0]
  if (int_pin == self.INT2):
    # bit=1 for INT2, set bit:
    int_map |= interrupt
  else:
    # bit=0 for INT1, clear bit:
    int_map &= ~interrupt
    self.i2c.write(self.addr, [0x2F, int_map])

    # Enable the interrupt
    int_enable = self.i2c.readTransaction(self.addr, 0x2E, 1)[0]
    int_enable |= interrupt # 1 to enable interrupt
    self.i2c.write(self.addr, [0x2E, int_enable])

def enable_tap_detection(self):
  # Enable taps for the different axes:
  self.i2c.write(self.addr, [0x2A, 0x7])
  self.set_tap_threshold(3) # 3g threshold
```

```
        self.set_tap_duration(20) # 20ms minimum duration
        self.set_tap_latency(100) # 100ms double-tap latency
        self.set_tap_window(1000) # 1s double-tap window

    def set_tap_threshold(self, threshold):
        # Convert to bits:
        threshold /= 0.0625
        # Round to nearest integer:
        threshold = int(threshold + 0.5)
        # Constrain to single byte:
        if threshold > 255: threshold = 255
        self.i2c.write(self.addr, [0x1D, threshold])

    def set_tap_duration(self, duration):
        duration /= 0.625
        duration = int(duration + 0.5)
            if duration > 255: duration = 255
            self.i2c.write(self.addr, [0x21, duration])

    def set_tap_latency(self, latency):
        latency /= 1.25
        latency = int(latency + 0.5)
        if latency > 255: latency = 255
        self.i2c.write(self.addr, [0x22, latency])

    def set_tap_window(self, window):
        window /= 1.25
        window = int(window + 0.5)
        if window > 255: window = 255
        self.i2c.write(self.addr, [0x23, window])

    def get_interrupts(self):
        # Read and return INT_SOURCE register:
        return self.i2c.readTransaction(self.addr, 0x30, 1)[0]
```

To use the tap detection, you'll need to configure and enable it, then set up some digital interrupts using PyBBIO to catch the changes on the INT pins. First connect the INT1 and INT2 outputs to GPIO3_14 (P8.31) and GPIO3_15 (P8.29), respectively:

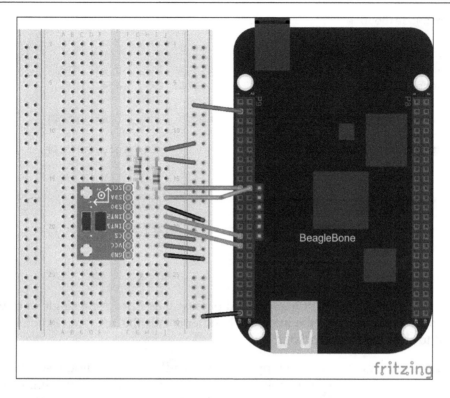

Then add the interrupt code to the main program:

```
from bbio import *
from adxl345 import ADXL345

accel = ADXL345(Wire2)
single_tap_pin = GPIO3_15 # INT2
double_tap_pin = GPIO3_14 # INT1

def tap_interrupt(taps):
  if taps == 1:
    print "Single tap detected"
  elif taps == 2:
    print "Double tap detected"
    accel.get_interrupts()

def setup():
  accel.begin()
  accel.set_range(accel.RANGE_8G)
  pinMode(single_tap_pin, INPUT)
```

```
    pinMode(double_tap_pin, INPUT)

    accel.enable_tap_detection()
    accel.enable_interrupt(accel.INT_SINGLE_TAP, accel.INT2)
    accel.enable_interrupt(accel.INT_DOUBLE_TAP, accel.INT1)

    attachInterrupt(double_tap_pin, lambda : tap_interrupt(2),
        RISING)
    attachInterrupt(single_tap_pin, lambda : tap_interrupt(1),
        RISING)

def loop():
    x, y, z = accel.get_xyz()
    print "X: {:0.2f}g, Y: {:0.2f}g, Z: {:0.2f}g".format(x,y,z)
    delay(1000)

run(setup, loop)
```

We're using a single interrupt handler and passing it as 1 or 2 for a single or double tap event, and at the end of the interrupt handler it calls the `get_interrupts()` method to clear the status register.

If you run the program and start tapping your breadboard, you should see the tap messages appearing. You'll probably notice that the double tap event is immediately followed by one or two single tap events, which is a product of the tap detection algorithm in the `ADXL345` class. This could be a problem in a case where a single and double tap are meant to be two distinct program inputs, but it can be worked around pretty simply by recording the time of each event and ignoring particular events based on how soon they follow the previous event. To show this method in action, here's a program that will let you turn on the USR3 LED with a single tap and turn it off with a double tap:

```
from bbio import *
from adxl345 import ADXL345

accel = ADXL345(Wire2)
single_tap_pin = GPIO3_15 # INT2
double_tap_pin = GPIO3_14 # INT1

# Time in ms to force between events:
event_holdoff = 750

last_event = {
    "time" : 0, # event timestamp
    "taps" : 1, # 1 for single, 2 for double
```

```
    "is_pending" : False # True if event is new
    }

def tap_interrupt(taps):
  event_time = millis() # time since program start in ms

  if event_time - last_event["time"] >= event_holdoff:
    # Greater than event_holdoff since last event,
    # save event and mark as pending:
    last_event["time"] = event_time
    last_event["taps"] = taps
    last_event["is_pending"] = True

  elif taps == 2:
    # A double tap event always overwrites a nearby single
    # tap event:
    last_event["time"] = event_time
    last_event["taps"] = taps
    last_event["is_pending"] = True

    accel.get_interrupts()

def setup():
  accel.begin()
  accel.set_range(accel.RANGE_8G)
  pinMode(single_tap_pin, INPUT)
  pinMode(double_tap_pin, INPUT)

  accel.enable_tap_detection()
  accel.enable_interrupt(accel.INT_SINGLE_TAP, accel.INT2)
  accel.enable_interrupt(accel.INT_DOUBLE_TAP, accel.INT1)

  attachInterrupt(double_tap_pin, lambda : tap_interrupt(2),
    RISING)
  attachInterrupt(single_tap_pin, lambda : tap_interrupt(1),
    RISING)

def loop():
  if last_event["is_pending"]:
    taps = last_event["taps"]
    if taps == 1:
      print "single tap, USR3 on"
      digitalWrite(USR3, HIGH)
    else:
```

```
        print "double tap, USR3 off"
        digitalWrite(USR3, LOW)

        # Clear it so as not to respond to it again the next
        # time through the loop:
        last_event["is_pending"] = False
    delay(100)

run(setup, loop)
```

This program could be expanded to control any number of things with taps, such as turning lights on and off, starting and stopping music, scrolling through a user interface on an LCD, and much more.

Summary

In this chapter, you learned the process required for interfacing with a new device, in this case the ADXL345 accelerometer, including how its I2C protocol works, how to configure and use its built-in tap detection, and how you can write a Python module to abstract away the interface code.

In the next chapter, we'll be looking at using the network connection to create web-based user interfaces for data streaming and remote control.

9

Using the Network

In this chapter, you will learn about using the BeagleBone's network connection to stream data to web services and control hardware remotely through web interfaces. We will cover the following topics:

- TCP/IP and TCP servers for remote hardware access
- HTTP servers for remote hardware access
- Streaming data to remote storage and visualization services

TCP/IP

The BeagleBone has an Ethernet, or IEEE 802.3, connection. This provides a physical layer over which TCP/IP is implemented. TCP/IP, or Transmission Control Protocol/Internet Protocol, is a suite of networking layers that makes up the base of what we call the Internet. It is named after its two most important layers, TCP, which provides error-checked data transfer between endpoints, and IP, which provides routing of packets between hosts based on their IP addresses.

Pretty much all modern operating systems provide interfaces called network sockets, which are created and used to abstract an Internet connection using a model like TCP/IP. A socket is defined by its protocol (for example, TCP), its local IP address, and its local port number. A port is a software abstraction that allows any number of processes on a computer with a single IP address to exchange data over the network independently of each other, by each having their own unique ID, called a port number. Once a connection has been made to a remote host, the socket also has the additional characteristics of the remote IP address and port.

Software implementing TCP/IP typically follows a server/client model. The server process has an open socket listening on a predefined port, and the client processes make connections to the server using its IP address and that port. For example, imagine there was a TCP server, with IP address 192.168.0.10, listening on port 8000. A client could then open a connection to the server, which would create a new socket on the server computer, characterized by the local address, 192.168.0.10:8000 (it is a common notation to append the port to the address, separated by a colon), as well as the client computers IP address and port. If a second client then opens a connection to the server, since the second client has a different address (even if it's the same IP address, it will have a different port number), a new socket will be created on the server computer. So, because the socket abstraction includes the local and remote addresses, it allows multiple connections from the same local port, which is the basis of the server/client model.

Python's built-in `socket` library provides an API for using these socket interfaces. Let's look at an example of a simple TCP server:

```
import socket

server = socket.socket(socket.AF_INET, socket.SOCK_STREAM)
server.bind(("", 8080))
server.listen(5)
while True:
  client, address = server.accept()
  print "incoming connection from", address
  data = client.recv(1024)
  if data:
    print "received data: {}".format(data)
    print "echoing data"
    client.send(data)
  client.close()
```

The call to `socket.socket()` creates a network socket and returns a Python object that abstracts it. The `AF_INET` argument tells it to use the Internet Protocol (IP) and `SOCK_STREAM` tells it to use the TCP transport. The empty string in the tuple passed to `bind()` tells it to auto-detect the local IP address, and `8080` is the local port to listen on. Passing `5` to `listen()` tells it to limit the number of simultaneous connections to port 8080 to 5.

Once the socket is set up and the program enters the while loop, the `server.accept()` method blocks the program until a new client connects, then it returns a new socket object representing the socket created for that connection as well as an address tuple in the same format passed to `bind()`. The `client.recv(1024)` call then blocks the program until a TCP data stream is sent by the client, and then it receives and returns up to 1024 bytes of it. We then print the data and echo it back to the client. If a new client connects while the program is still connected to a client and receiving data, a new object socket will be created for the new connection. When the program then loops back to the `server.accept()` method, a new socket object representing the new connection will be returned immediately. The limit of 5 sockets that we set previously with the `listen()` method is the maximum number of sockets that can be created; in this non-threaded server, we only ever have a single socket object handling a single client at a time.

With your server running, you can use the `netcat` command line tool to connect to it as a client. First make sure you have `netcat` installed:

```
# apt-get update && apt-get install netcat
```

Then connect to the server:

```
# netcat localhost 8000
```

You can then start typing characters into `netcat`, and when you press *Enter* it will send the string in a TCP/IP packet to the server:

```
root@beaglebone:~# netcat localhost 5000
localhost [127.0.0.1] 5000 (?) : Connection refused
root@beaglebone:~# netcat localhost 8000
Hello, World!
Hello, World!
root@beaglebone:~#
```

```
imcoming connection from ('127.0.0.1', 52695)
received data: Hello, World!

echoing data
```

You can also use `netcat` from another Linux machine on the same network by replacing 'localhost' with your BeagleBone's IP address. You can use PuTTY to connect from a Windows machine on the same network by setting it to use Telnet in passive mode (meaning it won't send any data until you've pressed *Enter*). To do so, select the **Telnet** section under **Connection** and select the **Passive** option:

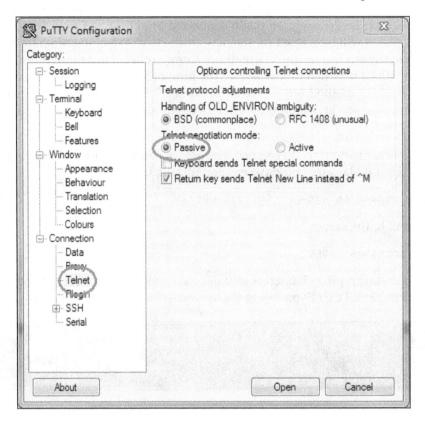

Then, back in the **Session** section, ensure **Telnet** is selected for the connection type, and enter the IP and port number:

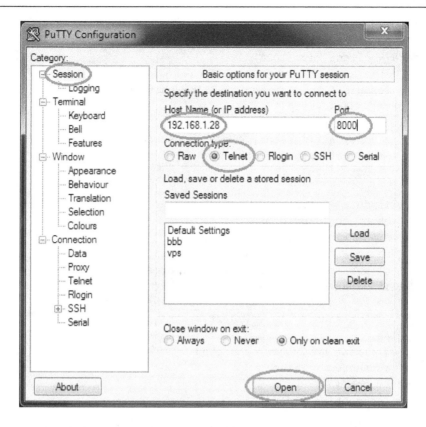

When you press **Open**, you'll see a blank terminal window that you can type into, and when you press *Enter*, it will send the data to the server. The window will close automatically because the server closes the connection after the first exchange of data, but it's easy to change the server code to maintain the connection until the client disconnects, as shown in the next example.

Now, let's extend the TCP server to allow remote hardware control:

```
import socket, bbio

server = socket.socket(socket.AF_INET, socket.SOCK_STREAM)
server.bind(("", 8000))
server.listen(5)
while True:
  print "waiting for client to connect"
  client, address = server.accept()
  print "incoming  connection from", address
```

```
connected = True
while connected:
  data = client.recv(1024)
  if data:
    # Strip off leading and trailing whitespace:
    data = data.strip()
    if data == "":
      # empty string sent, close connection
      print "closing connection"
      client.close()
      break
    elif data == "toggle":
      bbio.toggle(bbio.USR3)
      state = bbio.pinState(bbio.USR3)
      state = "High" if state else "Low"
      client.send("  USR3 : {}\r\n".format(state))
    elif data == "analogRead":
      volts = bbio.inVolts(bbio.analogRead(bbio.AIN0))
      client.send("  A0 : {:0.2f}V\r\n".format(volts))
    else:
      # client no longer connected
      connected = False
client.close()
print "connection closed"
```

If you connect to this server remotely using netcat or PuTTY, you can send the string toggle to toggle the USR3 LED, or the string analogRead to get the voltage on the AIN0 pin:

```
root@beaglebone:~# netcat localhost 8000
toggle
  USR3 : Low
toggle
  USR3 : High
analogRead
  A0 : 1.70V

```

HTTP

HTTP, or Hypertext Transfer Protocol, is an application protocol that's implemented on top of the TCP/IP suite, and is what the **World Wide Web (WWW)** is built on. The HTTP protocol defines the request-response structure, in which a client (such as a web browser) requests a resource from a server whose address is given by a **Uniform Resource Locator (URL)**, and the server responds with a resource, such as an HTML file. So instead of opening a TCP socket and keeping it open while passing raw TCP/IP packets, as in the preceding example, the HTTP client connects to the server over a TCP socket and sends an HTTP request packet, then the server sends back an HTTP response packet, and the socket is closed.

PyBBIO includes a library called `BBIOServer`, which provides an API for creating simple HTML pages for web based user interfaces using HTTP. Let's run a simple example:

```
from bbio import *
from bbio.libraries.BBIOServer import BBIOServer, Page

server = BBIOServer(8000)

def setup():
  page1 = Page("Server Test")
  page1.add_text("Testing the BBIOServer library")

  page2 = Page("LED Control")
  page2.add_text("Control an on-board LED)

  page2.add_button(lambda: toggle(USR3), "Toggle USR3 LED",
    newline=True)
  page2.add_monitor(lambda: pinState(USR3), "current state:")

  server.start(page1, page2)

def loop():
  print "\nServer has stopped, exiting"
  stop()

run(setup, loop)
```

The Page class is used to build an HTML file, where each Page instance defines an individual web page. This example shows the button element, which creates an HTML button that sends a signal to the server when pressed, telling it to call the provided function; it also creates the monitor element, which routinely sends requests to the server, triggering it to call the provided function and return the result, which is then put into a text field on the page. The dynamic nature of the page is achieved using some predefined JavaScript functions, and the library includes a CSS stylesheet to format and color the page.

The BBIOServer class contains the HTTP server code. Once built, the Page instances are passed to its start() method so it knows what resources it has to send to clients, then it starts listening on the port that it was passed when initialized.

You can run the preceding example and navigate to the server (for example, if your BeagleBone's IP address is 192.168.1.28, it would be http://192.168.1.28:8000), you'll see the site and you'll be able to control the USR3 LED:

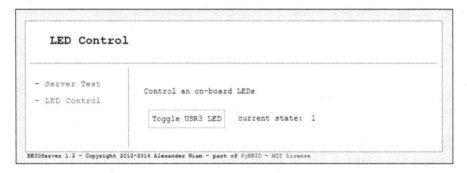

 For more information on BBIOServer, check out the documentation and tutorials at https://github.com/graycatlabs/PyBBIO/wiki/BBIOServer.

It's important to note that there are many potential security concerns when connecting a device to the Internet, and BBIOserver makes no effort to address them. It is only recommended to use BBIOserver on a trusted network, and it shouldn't be made accessible from outside that local network.

IoT Services

There are a number of services targeting the Internet of Things market that provide a place to store and view data over the Internet. These services typically include a simple HTTP API for streaming data to them, as well as a web interface for viewing the stored data, both as raw samples and in various visual ways. The idea is that you'd have a device like a BeagleBone on a local network, say at your home, and it would be routinely sampling some sort of sensor, say measuring temperature. Every time it reads a new temperature value, the BeagleBone will send it to the remote service's database over the Internet. Then you would be able to go to a website from anywhere, say if you were traveling, and look at the current temperature in your home, as well as track your home's temperature in the past. This is not the most exciting example, but even this could be practical as you could know right away if your heating has stopped working, and you could call to have it serviced before your pipes freeze.

Phant

SparkFun electronics provide a very basic data stream hosting service called Phant, which can be found at `http://phant.io`. You can install the Phant server on your own computer, and they even have a tutorial for installing it on a BeagleBone, so it can store data locally from itself and from other sensors on the same network. They also maintain an instance of it running on their own servers, and anyone can create a stream on it to store and view their data. To create a stream, you'll need to go to `https://data.sparkfun.com/streams/make` and fill out the form describing your stream.

The data is stored in Phant's database as a table, where each row is a time-stamped sample, and the **Fields** section defines the columns in the table. In this example, I've only created a single column called `voltage`, but you could have multiple columns to store data from different sensors in the same stream; for example, you could have a weather station stream with temperature, humidity, and pressure columns:

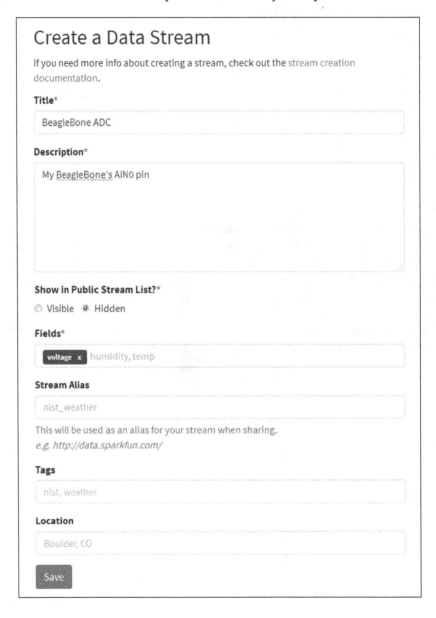

Once you click on the **Save** button, you will be brought to a page that gives you your stream's **Public Key**, **Private Key**, and **Delete Key**. It's up to you to store all of these, and if you lose them, your stream will no longer be accessible.

Data is sent to the Phant server as a type of HTTP request called a POST request, which, as its name implies, is meant for posting data to a server. The POST request packet sent includes the Phant Public Key, which identifies the stream you want to use, the Phant Private Key, which authenticates you to write to the stream, and the data to write, organized into the fields.

It's easy to assemble a request packet for Phant in Python using the requests library (`http://docs.python-requests.org`), which provides an API aimed at making it easy to send HTTP requests. First, make sure the library is installed:

```
# pip install requests
```

Now, we can write a program that uses `Adafruit_BBIO` to send ADC readings to your new Phant stream every second:

```
import Adafruit_BBIO.ADC as ADC
import requests, time

PUBLIC_KEY = "q580YQ7mW8IJbdVLaQLo"
PRIVATE_KEY = "BVeW4XZg9eiP1Bgzw7zY"

def postData(data_dict):
  url = "http://data.sparkfun.com/input/{}".format(PUBLIC_KEY)
  headers = {"Phant-Private-Key" : PRIVATE_KEY}
  response = requests.post(url, headers=headers,
    params=data_dict)

ADC.setup()
try:
  while True:
    voltage = ADC.read("AIN0") * 1.8
    postData({"voltage" : voltage})
    time.sleep(1)
except KeyboardInterrupt:
  pass
```

You'll need to replace the `PUBLIC_KEY` and `PRIVATE_KEY` values with the keys you were given when you created your stream, and since this example is using `Adafruit_BBIO`, you'll want to be sure to enable the ADC Device Tree overlay before you run it (as described in *Chapter 4, PWM and ADC Subsystems*):

```
# echo BB-ADC > /sys/devices/bone_capemgr.*/slots
```

Once the program is running, you can go to your stream view at `https://data.sparkfun.com/streams/PUBLIC_KEY`:

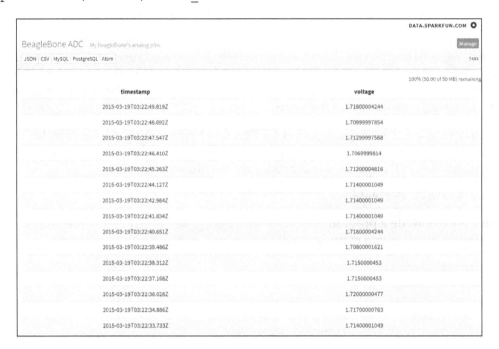

 Your private key can be used to delete the channel, so be sure not to share it with anyone unless you trust them with that power.

Phant doesn't include any sort of visualization, but it does let you download the data in various formats, including CSV, which you can open in any spreadsheet program and create plots from it.

dweet.io

Another service similar to `https://data.sparkfun.com` is dweet.io (`http://dweet.io`). As with Phant, dweet.io can store the data from your devices, and, along with letting you view the raw data, it also provides some basic live plots. The API is simpler than Phant's, with only a user-defined name distinguishing your data stream, which `dweet.io` calls a *thing*, from others instead of a public/private API key pair. There's no setup required for dweet.io, you simply make an HTTP request with your data and thing name, and it does the rest. If a thing by that name doesn't exist, the channel is created, automatically.

While this method makes it easier to get set up and start sending data, it also means that if you call your thing BeagleBone on dweet.io, and someone else calls their thing BeagleBone as well, the two data streams will interfere with each other. To avoid this scenario, it's best to include a **universally unique identifier (UUID)** in your thing names to ensure that they are unique. It's easy to generate a UUID in Python with the built-in uuid module. Fire up the Python interpreter and generate a random UUID:

```
root@beaglebone:~# python
Python 2.7.3 (default, Mar 14 2014, 17:55:54)
[GCC 4.6.3] on linux2
Type "help", "copyright", "credits" or "license" for more information.
>>> import uuid
>>> uuid.uuid4()
UUID('7f51dd9d-09e9-43a0-ab42-ed55b46f21ea')
```

Save that string in a file somewhere you won't lose it. You could create a new UUID for each of your dweet.io things, but it's probably less confusing to consider that one UUID as your identifier and to append a plain-text name to the end, for example, 7f51dd9d-09e9-43a0-ab42-ed55b46f21ea_BeagleBone-temperature.

Using the requests library again, it only takes a few lines of code to send data to dweet.io:

```
import requests

def dweet(thing, **vals):
  url = "http://dweet.io/dweet/for/{}".format(thing)
  requests.post(url, params=vals)
```

This function takes the thing name as well as key-value pairs of data.

> If you've never seen the **vals notation before, it allows you to call a function with any number of named values and they will be put into a dictionary object, for example, if you define the function:
>
> ```
> def foo(**kwargs):
>     # do something with kwargs here
> ```
>
> When you called it with foo(val1=3, val2="string"), you would end up with the dictionary {"val1" : 3, "val2" : "string"} stored in the kwargs variable.

So, for example, if you were to call dweet("my-thing-name", temperature=25), the result would be a HTTP POST request to http://dweet.io/dweet/for/my-thing-name?temperature=25.

Let's revisit the system monitor idea we used in *Chapter 6, Program Output,* to show dweet.io in action:

```python
import requests, psutil, datetime

# Replace "x" sequence with your UUID:
thing_name = "xxxxxxxx-xxxx-xxxx-xxxx-xxxxxxxxxxxx_BeagleBone"

def dweet(thing, **vals):
    url = "http://dweet.io/dweet/for/{}".format(thing)
    requests.post(url, params=vals)

def get_cpu_temp_c():
    temp_file = "/sys/class/hwmon/hwmon0/device/temp1_input"
    with open(temp_file, "r") as f:
        return int(f.read())/1000

def get_uptime():
    with open("/proc/uptime", "r") as f:
        raw = f.read()
    seconds = float(raw.split()[0])
    return seconds

while True:
    uptime_s = get_uptime()
    uptime_datetime = datetime.datetime.fromtimestamp(uptime_s)
    uptime = uptime_datetime.strftime("%H:%M:%S")

    load = psutil.cpu_percent(interval=2)
    temp = get_cpu_temp_c()
    mem = psutil.virtual_memory()[2]
    net_info = psutil.net_io_counters()
    eth_up = net_info[2]
    eth_down = net_info[3]

    dweet(thing_name, uptime=uptime, cpu_load=load, cpu_temp=temp,
        memory=mem, eth_up=eth_up, eth_down=eth_down)
```

We're reusing a lot of the code from the LCD-based system monitor, with the addition of a new `get_uptime()` function, which returns the number of seconds since the last time your BeagleBone Black powered on. We're then using the `datetime` library to convert it to a string in the friendlier `HH:MM:SS` form.

Be sure to fill in your UUID in the `thing_name` string, then run the program.
Now if you head over to `http://dweet.io/follow/xxxxxxxx-xxxx-xxxx-xxxx-`
`xxxxxxxxxxxx_BeagleBone` (filling in your UUID) you should see a live plot of
your data:

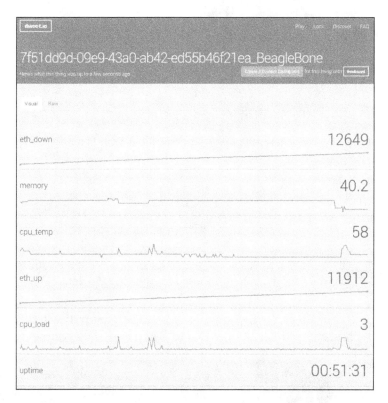

You could simply add an entry to your `crontab` file to start this program at boot,
as described in *Chapter 3, Digital Outputs*, and you'd be able to see your BeagleBone
Black's system resources in real time from anywhere. With the added uptime value,
you'd also know if your BeagleBone had rebooted unexpectedly, due to a power
outage, for example.

Freeboard

Freeboard (`https://freeboard.io/`) is a data visualization tool. It is a paid service,
but it allows you to have public dashboards for free. In other words, you pay to
use your private data. Freeboard doesn't provide data storage of its own, rather it
provides you with a visual dashboard that you can plug into various data sources,
including dweet.io things.

Once you've created an account at `https://freeboard.io/signup`, you can create a new Freeboard by entering a name and pressing **Create New**:

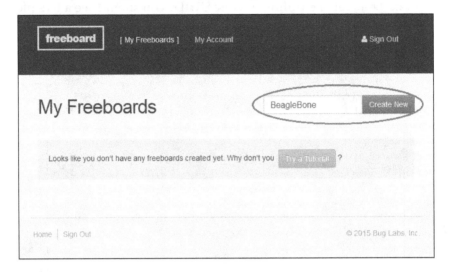

 Each Freeboard is a separate container for a set of data streams as well as a separate dashboard for viewing the data.

When you create your Freeboard, you will automatically be redirected to its empty dashboard. The first step is to click on **ADD** to add a new data source:

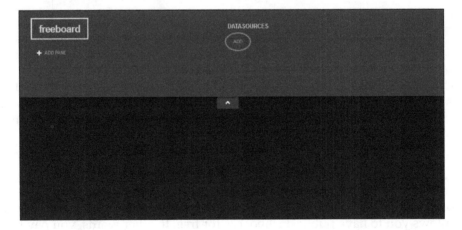

We'll connect this Freeboard to the system monitor dweet.io thing we just made; in the window that pops up, first select **Dweet.io** from the drop-down, then give it a friendly name, and fill in the dweet.io thing name (once again using your own UUID):

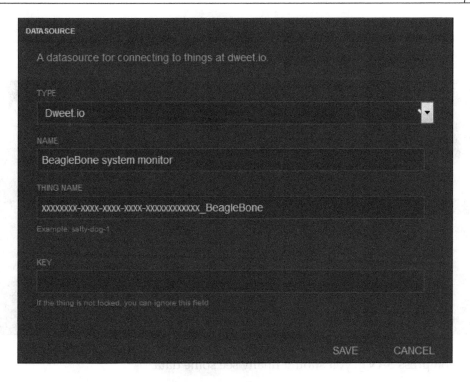

Don't worry when you don't see any data after you press **SAVE**, we still need to configure the displays. The Freeboard consists of visual blocks called panes, which contain display objects called widgets. Each widget connects to a single data channel and displays its data in one of a number of selectable formats, and the separate panes can be rearranged on the dashboard. To get some data displayed, first click on **ADD PANE** and then on the plus sign on the pane that appears to add a new widget:

In the widget configuration box that pops up, select the **Text** type, enable the **INCLUDE SPARKLINE** switch, and use the **+DATASOURCE** button to select the **cpu_load** channel of your BeagleBone system monitor source:

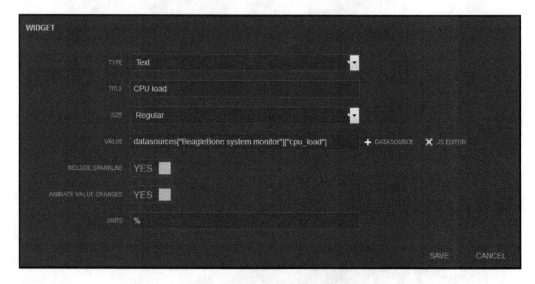

Once you press **SAVE**, you should finally see some data:

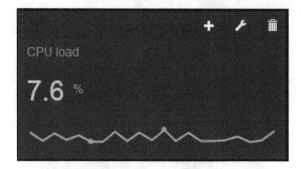

Take some time to play around with the other widget types; for instance, the gauge widget is a good choice for something like CPU load that has a fixed upper boundary:

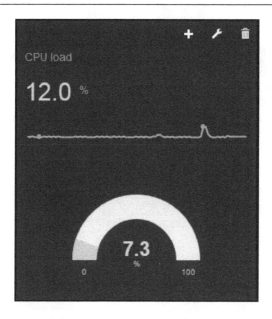

With a little work, you can put together a great-looking custom dashboard for your data:

Summary

In this chapter, you learned how to take advantage of the BeagleBone's network connection to communicate with external hardware remotely, as well as to stream data to remote servers for storage and viewing.

In the next chapter, we will build upon what you've learned throughout the book to create some larger and more useful programs.

10
A Practical Example

In this chapter, you will use what you've learned throughout the book to build a complete, practical application. We will cover the following topics:

- Building a simple weather station
- Getting the weather data online
- Implementing weather alerts
- Creating a web interface for configuring the alerts

Weather station

Until this point, we've only looked at relatively simple program examples, without any real scope to them. Let's take some time to build a more complete program that actually accomplishes a practical task, a weather station.

Let's start with the hardware. We'll use a HTU21D I2C relative humidity sensor (for example, `https://www.sparkfun.com/products/12064`), as well as a BMP183 SPI pressure sensor (for example, `https://www.adafruit.com/product/1900`). Both include internal temperature sensors from which we can retrieve data, so we won't need an additional temperature sensor.

For this circuit, you will need:

- Breadboard
- 1x HTU21D breakout board
- 1x BMP183 breakout board
- Jumper wires

Wire up the breakout boards as shown:

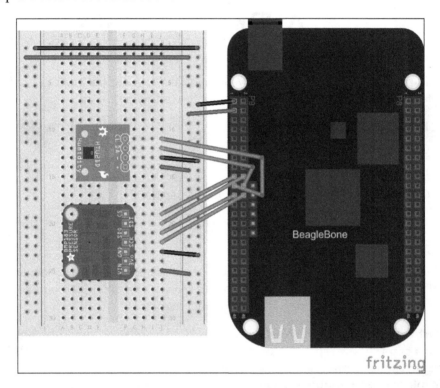

PyBBIO includes libraries for both sensors, so we'll use it for this program. For starters, let's look at getting the data from the sensors:

```
from bbio import *
from bbio.libraries.BMP183 import BMP183
from bbio.libraries.HTU21D import HTU21D

bmp = BMP183(SPI0)
```

```
htu = HTU21D(I2C2)

def setup():
  pass

def loop():
  pressure = bmp.getPressure() # in Pascals
  rh = htu.getHumidity() # in %RH
  temp = htu.getTemp() # in Celsius
  dew_point = htu.calculateDewPoint(rh, temp) # in Celsius
  pressure /= 1000.0 # convert Pa to kPa

  print "temperature : {:0.2f} C".format(temp)
  print "humidity    : {:0.2f} %RH".format(rh)
  print "pressure    : {:0.2f} kPa".format(pressure)
  print "dew point   : {:0.2f} C\n".format(dew_point)
  delay(3000)

run(setup, loop)
```

Connecting to the Internet

The PyBBIO libraries make it pretty straightforward to get the data, but we want to be able to view the weather remotely, so printing it to the terminal isn't going to cut it. There are a number of services that provide data storage and remote viewing for your connected devices; we'll use ThingSpeak (`https://thingspeak.com/`), which provides free data storage and plotting. The benefit of using a service like ThingSpeak is that you don't need to set up things, such as port forwarding in order to make your BeagleBone directly accessible from the Internet, which comes with certain security risks.

You'll need to start by setting up a ThingSpeak account at `https://thingspeak.com/users/sign_up`. Once you've logged into your account, navigate to **My Channels** in the **Channel** menu of the top menu bar and press the **Create Channel** button. You'll need to give the channel a name, and then fill in the first four of the available fields for the data created in the previous program, as shown in the following screenshot:

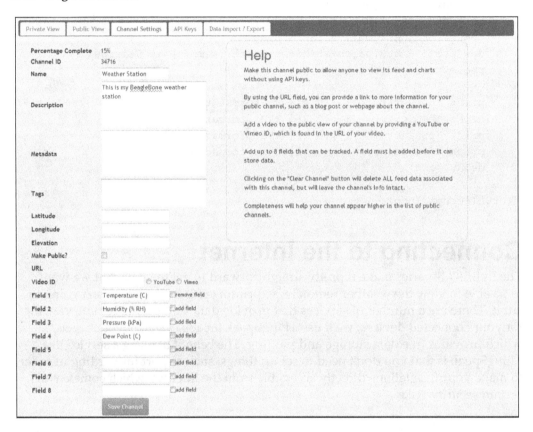

Once you press **Save Channel**, you'll be brought straight to **Private View**, where you should see four empty plots. This is where you'll be able to view your data live as it's sent by the weather station.

ThingSpeak provides a friendly HTTP API, making it simple to send data from any device with an Internet connection. PyBBIO's IoT library includes a `ThingSpeakChannel` class built on top of that API. However, before your program can send data to your channel, you'll need to get its API key, which is used to authenticate your POST requests so that ThingSpeak knows what channel it's going to. This is easily found on the **API Keys** tab of your channel under **Write API Key**, as shown in the following screenshot:

The IoT library uses the `requests` module, so make sure it's installed on your BeagleBone:

```
# pip install requests
```

Let's revise the previous program to send the data to your ThingSpeak channel instead of to the terminal:

```python
from bbio import *
from bbio.libraries.BMP183 import BMP183
from bbio.libraries.HTU21D import HTU21D
from bbio.libraries.IoT import thingspeak

API_KEY = "3FYOJN7XYD8Y0MYV"

bmp = BMP183(SPI0)
htu = HTU21D(I2C2)
channel = thingspeak.ThingSpeakChannel(API_KEY)

def setup():
    pass

def loop():
    pressure = bmp.getPressure() / 1000.0 # in kPa
    rh = htu.getHumidity()
    temp = htu.getTemp()
    dew_point = htu.calculateDewPoint(rh, temp)
    channel.post([temp, rh, pressure, dew_point])

    delay(30000)

run(setup, loop)
```

Be sure to replace the API key with your correct one. Note that instead of sampling the sensors every 3 seconds, this time, we delay 30 seconds between samples; since the idea of the weather station is to monitor the weather over a long period of time, and since the weather doesn't tend to change drastically within a 30 second span, this will help limit network traffic while still providing a good resolution.

If you leave that program running and watch the ThingSpeak channel view, you should start to see your data appear, as shown in the following screenshot:

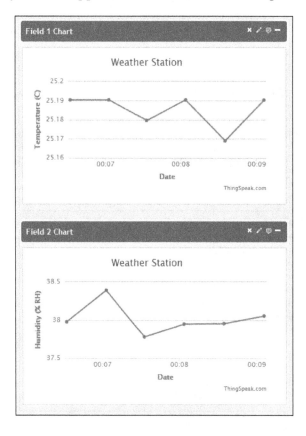

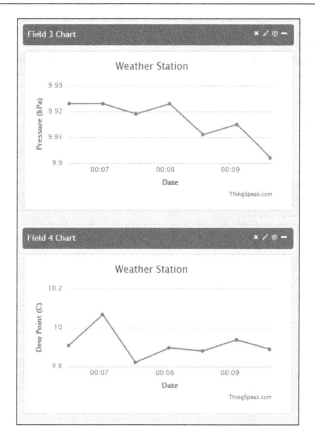

So already you have a way to see the current weather wherever your BeagleBone is, as well as historical weather trends, from anywhere with Internet access. But let's not stop there.

Weather alerts

One great application for this sort of small, relatively low-cost, and Internet connected weather station is the ability to get alerts. For instance, if you live in a cold area, you could get an alert if your heating system has stopped working and your water pipes are at risk of freezing and bursting. We already looked at sending e-mails in *Chapter 6, Program Output*, so we'll use that same code for notifications.

To implement alarms, we'll also want a way to configure their thresholds and to enable and disable them. For this, we'll use BBIOServer to build a quick web UI. This will let you configure alarms while on the same local network as your BeagleBone, so you would setup your alarms before leaving your house, for example.

You can also display your ThingSpeak plots right in a BBIOServer page (or any webpage) by using their provided embed HTML.

To get the embed code, click on the button that looks like a message box at the top right of each plot you want to embed; the HTML will be provided in the box that pops up, as shown in the following screenshot:

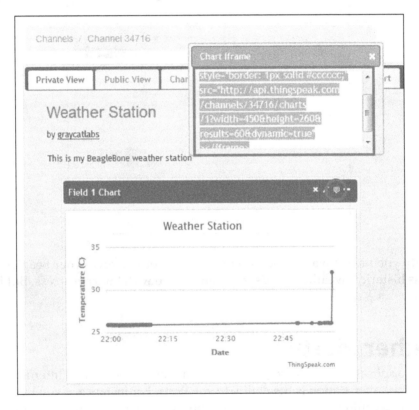

If you have not made your channel private, the embed code won't work as is, but you can make it work by adding the API key to a new `key` parameter at the end of the source URL, for example:

```
<iframe width="450" height="260" style="border: 1px solid #cccccc;"
        src="http://api.thingspeak.com/channels/34716/
charts/%i?width=450&
```

```
                    height=260&results=60&dynamic=true&key=3FYOJN7XYD8Y0M
YV" >
</iframe>
```

We're now ready to build the new and improved weather station:

```
from bbio import *
from bbio.libraries.BMP183 import BMP183
from bbio.libraries.HTU21D import HTU21D
from bbio.libraries.IoT import thingspeak
from bbio.libraries.BBIOServer import BBIOServer, Page

import smtplib
from email.mime.text import MIMEText

THINGSPEAK_API_KEY = "3FYOJN7XYD8Y0MYV"

bmp = BMP183(SPI0)
htu = HTU21D(I2C2)
channel = thingspeak.ThingSpeakChannel(THINGSPEAK_API_KEY)
server = BBIOServer(blocking=False)
# We start the server in non-blocking mode with blocking=False,
# which let's the main loop continue to sample the sensors while
# it serves the web site in the background.

# The details for the sending account:
SMTP_host = "smtp.gmail.com"
SMTP_email = "username@gmail.com"
SMTP_pass = "password"
# The address to send alerts to:
to_email = "username@example.com" # could be an SMS proxy as well!

# This HTML chunk is used to embed the ThingSpeak plots into the
# BBIOServer page:
embedded_plot = \
"""
<iframe width="450" height="260" style="border: 1px solid
  #cccccc;"
    src="http://api.thingspeak.com/channels/34716/charts/{}?width=450&
      height=260&results=60&dynamic=true&key=3FYOJN7XYD8Y0MYV">
</iframe>
"""
```

```python
# This stores the weather data. It's global so it's accessible from the
# BBIOServer callbacks
weather_data = {
    "temperature" : 0,
    "humidity" : 0,
    "pressure" : 0,
    "dew_point" : 0
    }


# This stores the alarm information. It's global so it's accessible from
# the BBIOServer callbacks
alarms = {
    "over_temp" : {
        "threshold" : 40,
        "enabled" : False,
        "tripped" : False,
        "description" : "Over temperature"
        },
    "under_temp" : {
        "threshold" : 0,
        "enabled" : False,
        "tripped" : False,
        "description" : "Under temperature"
        }
    }

def send_email(to, subject, body):
    msg = MIMEText(body)
    msg["Subject"] = subject
    msg["From"] = SMTP_email
    msg["To"] = to
    server = smtplib.SMTP_SSL(SMTP_host)
    try:
        server.login(SMTP_email, SMTP_pass)
        server.sendmail(SMTP_email, to, msg.as_string())
    except smtplib.SMTPAuthenticationError:
        print "warning: cannot login to email server!"

def alarm(trigger):
    """ Creates and sends the appropriate email for the given
        trigger. """
    body = "{} alert\n".format(alarms[trigger]["description"])
```

```
    body += "Current weather:\n"
    body += "Temperature: {:0.2f}
        C\n".format(weather_data.get("temperature"))
    body += "Humidity: {:0.2f}
        %RH\n".format(weather_data.get("humidity"))
    body += "Pressure: {:0.2f}
        kPa\n".format(weather_data.get("pressure"))
    body += "Dew point: {:0.2f}
        C\n".format(weather_data.get("dew_point"))

    send_email(to_email, "Weather Alert", body)

###
# These functions are all BBIOServer callbacks to configure the
# thresholds and enabled/disabled states of the alarms
def toggle_over_temp():
    alarms["over_temp"]["enabled"] = \
        not alarms["over_temp"]["enabled"]


def over_temp_state():
    return "Enabled" if alarms["over_temp"]["enabled"] else
        "Disabled"


def toggle_under_temp():
    alarms["under_temp"]["enabled"] = \
        not alarms["under_temp"]["enabled"]


def under_temp_state():
    return "Enabled" if alarms["under_temp"]["enabled"] else
        "Disabled"


def set_over_temp(val):
    global alarms
    try:
        alarms["over_temp"]["threshold"] = float(val)
    except ValueError:
        pass


def setUnderTemp(val):
    global alarms
    try:
        alarms["under_temp"]["threshold"] = float(val)
    except ValueError:
        pass
```

```
###

def check_alarms(temp, rh, pressure, dew_point):
    """ Checks each value and triggers any appropriate enabled
       alarms. """
    if (alarms["over_temp"]["enabled"] and \
            temp > alarms["over_temp"]["threshold"]):
        if not alarms["over_temp"]["tripped"]:
            alarm("over_temp")
            alarms["over_temp"]["tripped"] = True
    else: alarms["over_temp"]["tripped"] = False

    if (alarms["under_temp"]["enabled"] and \
            temp < alarms["under_temp"]["threshold"]):
        if not alarms["under_temp"]["tripped"]:
            alarm("under_temp")
            alarms["under_temp"]["tripped"] = True
    else: alarms["under_temp"]["tripped"] = False


def setup():
    # Create a main page which displays the live plots:
    home_page = Page("Data")
    home_page.add_html(embedded_plot.format(1))
    home_page.add_html(embedded_plot.format(2))
    home_page.add_html("<br />")
    home_page.add_html(embedded_plot.format(3))
    home_page.add_html(embedded_plot.format(4))

    # Create a page for configuring the alarms:
    alarm_page = Page("Alarms")
    alarm_page.add_text("Over temp:")
    alarm_page.add_entry(set_over_temp, "set")
    alarm_page.add_monitor(lambda : alarms["over_temp"]["threshold"],
                           "Current:", units="C")
    alarm_page.add_button(toggle_over_temp, "toggle")
    alarm_page.add_monitor(over_temp_state, "")

    alarm_page.add_text("Under temp:", newline=True)
    alarm_page.add_entry(setUnderTemp, "set")
    alarm_page.add_monitor(lambda : alarms["under_temp"]["threshold"],
                           "Current:", units="C")
```

```
        alarm_page.add_button(toggle_under_temp, "toggle")
        alarm_page.add_monitor(under_temp_state, "")

        # Create a page for viewing the raw data:
        raw_data = Page("Raw data")
        raw_data.add_monitor(
            lambda : "{:0.2f}".format(weather_data.get("temperature")),
            "Temperature:", units="C"
            )
        raw_data.add_monitor(
            lambda : "{:0.2f}".format(weather_data.get("humidity")),
            "Humidity:", units="%%RH", newline=True
            )
        raw_data.add_monitor(
            lambda : "{:0.2f}".format(weather_data.get("pressure")),
            "Pressure:", units="kPa", newline=True
            )
        raw_data.add_monitor(
            lambda : "{:0.2f}".format(weather_data.get("dew_point")),
            "Dew point:", units="C", newline=True
            )

        # Start the server:
        server.start(home_page, alarm_page, raw_data)

    def loop():
        global weather_data
        pressure = bmp.getPressure()/1000.0
        rh = htu.getHumidity()
        temp = htu.getTemp()
        dew_point = htu.calculateDewPoint(rh, temp)
        weather_data["pressure"] = pressure
        weather_data["humidity"] = rh
        weather_data["temperature"] = temp
        weather_data["dew_point"] = dew_point

        check_alarms(temp, rh, pressure, dew_point)

        channel.post([temp, rh, pressure, dew_point])
        delay(30000)

run(setup, loop)
```

If you run that and head on over to your BeagleBone's IP address at port `8000` (for example, `http://192.168.1.28:8000`), you should see your ThingSpeak plots moving along like so:

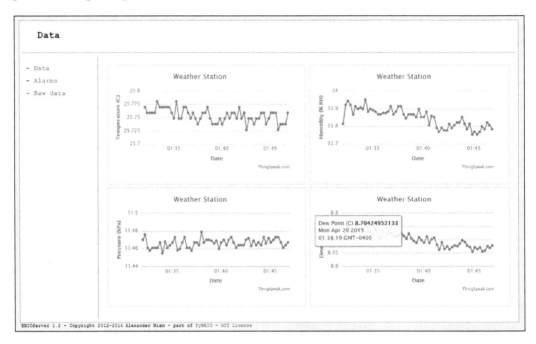

Navigate to the **Alarms** page, and you will be able to set over and under temperature thresholds, and enable e-mail alerts for each:

Finally, if a threshold is crossed you'll get an e-mail alert letting you know the current weather conditions:

```
to me ▾

Over temperature alert
Current weather:
Temperature: 25.28 C
Humidity: 37.37 %RH
Pressure: 9.89 kPa
Dew point: 9.74 C
```

Summary

In this final chapter, we put together a few of the concepts you learned throughout the book to build a weather station, complete with remote data viewing and configurable weather alerts. Hopefully, this gave you a better idea of how the tools you learned can help you quickly and easily build practical real-world devices with your BeagleBone Black.

The BeagleBone Black Pinout

This figure shows the pinouts of the **P8** and **P9** expansion headers on the BeagleBone Black, color-coded by subsystem. **P9** is shown on the left and **P8** is shown on the right, to match their physical orientation on the board:

P9				P8	
GND	1	2 GND	GND	1	2 GND
3.3V	3	4 3.3V	GPIO1_6	3	4 GPIO1_7
5V Raw	5	6 5V Raw	GPIO1_2	5	6 GPIO1_3
5V	7	8 5V	GPIO2_2	7	8 GPIO2_3
	9	10	GPIO2_5	9	10 GPIO2_4
Serial4_RX/GPIO0_30	11	12 GPIO1_28	eQEP2bB/GPIO1_13	11	12 GPIO1_12/eQEP2bA
Serial4_TX/GPIO0_31	13	14 GPIO1_18/PWM1A	PWM2B/GPIO0_23	13	14 GPIO0_26
GPIO1_16	15	16 GPIO1_19/PWM1B	GPIO1_15	15	16 GPIO1_14
I2C1_SCL/SPI0_CS0/GPIO0_5	17	18 GPIO0_4/SPI0_MOSI/I2C1_SDA	GPIO0_27	17	18 GPIO2_1
I2C2_SCL/GPIO0_13	19	20 GPIO0_12/I2C2_SDA	PWM2A/GPIO0_22	19	20 GPIO1_31
Serial2_TX/SPI0_MISO/GPIO0_3	21	22 GPIO0_2/Serial2_RX/SPI0_SCLK	GPIO1_30	21	22 GPIO1_5
GPIO1_17	23	24 GPIO0_15/Serial1_TX	GPIO1_4	23	24 GPIO1_1
GPIO3_21	25	26 GPIO0_14/Serial1_RX	GPIO1_0	25	26 GPIO1_29
eQEP0B/GPIO3_19	27	28 GPIO3_17/SPI1_CS0	GPIO2_22	27	28 GPIO2_24
SPI1_MISO/GPIO3_15	29	30 GPIO3_16/SPI1_MOSI	GPIO2_23	29	30 GPIO2_25
SPI1_SCLK/GPIO3_14	31	32 VDD_ADC	GPIO0_10	31	32 GPIO0_11
AIN4	33	34 GND_ADC	eQEP1B/GPIO0_9	33	34 GPIO2_17
AIN6	35	36 AIN5	eQEP1A/GPIO0_8	35	36 GPIO2_16
AIN2	37	38 AIN3	Serial5_TX/GPIO2_14	37	38 GPIO2_15/Serial5_RX
AIN0	39	40 AIN1	GPIO2_12	39	40 GPIO2_13
GPIO0_20	41	42 GPIO0_7/SPI1_CS1/eQEP0A	eQEP2A/GPIO2_10	41	42 GPIO2_11/eQEP2B
GND	43	44 GND	GPIO2_8	43	44 GPIO2_9
GND	45	46 GND	GPIO2_6	45	46 GPIO2_27

The pins with multiple functions can only be used for one thing at a time, for example, **PWM1A** shouldn't be used if **GPIO1_18** is already in use.

 Some pins on the P8 header are reserved for the HDMI output by default and can't be used without disabling HDMI. See Appendix B: Disabling HDMI for more info.

B

Disabling HDMI

The BeagleBone Black ships with the HDMI output enabled, using pins 20-46 on the P8 header. If you're not using HDMI and would like to free up those pins for use as shown in *Appendix A*, *The BeagleBone Black Pinout*, you can disable the HDMI output. First, mount the boot partition:

```
# mkdir /mnt/boot
# mount /dev/mmcblk0p1 /mnt/boot
```

Then, open the bootscript with the nano text editor:

```
# nano /mnt/boot/uEnv.txt
```

Add the following line to the end of the file:

```
optargs=quiet capemgr.disable_partno=BB-BONELT-HDMI,BB-BONELT-HDMIN
```

Press *Ctrl* + *X* then *Y* to save and close the file. That new line stops the capemgr driver from loading the HDMI, and HDMI audio overlays at boot, freeing up the pins for general use.

Finally, unmount the boot partition and reboot:

```
# umount /mnt/boot
# rmdir /mnt/boot
# reboot
```

The HDMI output will now be disabled, and you'll be able to use P8.20-46, as shown in *Appendix A*, *The BeagleBone Black Pinout*. To re-enable HDMI, repeat the steps and remove the line you added to uEnv.txt.

Index

Symbol

7-segment displays
about 82-85
URL 83

A

accelerometers
about 117
data, reading 119, 120
interfacing 118, 119
interrupts, using 124-132
module, writing 121-123
analog device
URL 119
analog-to-digital converter (ADC)
about 3, 49
voltage divider 49-51
voltage follower 52-54
analogWrite() function 42, 45
Arduino
URL 23

B

BBIOServer
URL 140
BeagleBone Black
analog-to-digital converter (ADC) 3
board, comparing 9
connecting, Cloud9 IDE used 14, 15
connecting, SSH used 15-17
connecting to 14
design 8

general purpose input/output (GPIO) 2
initial setup 11
overview 1, 2
pinout 169
resource links 10
tools and additional hardware 6-8
URL 1
button
about 59-61
circuit requisites 59
interrupts 70-72
polling 63-69
pull-up/pull-down resistors 61-63

C

character LCD 90-93
Cloud9 IDE
URL 14
used, for connecting to BeagleBone
Black 14, 15

D

Debian image
updating 12-14
URL 12
delay() function 25
Digi-Key
URL 6
dual in-line package (DIP) 52
duty cycle 42
dweet.io
about 144-147
URL 144

E

Ethernet
  used, for connecting to BeagleBone
     Black 17, 18

F

Farnel
  URL 7
Fing
  URL 18
Freeboard
  about 147-151
  URL 147

G

**general purpose input/output (GPIO)
    modules**
  about 2, 27
  kernel drivers 27, 28
  pin multiplexing 28, 29
GPIO pins
  higher currents, driving from 33-35

I

initial setup, BeagleBone Black
  steps 11, 12
interactive GPIO 29-32
Inter-Integrated Circuit (I2C) 6, 104-110
Internet
  connecting, Ethernet used 17, 18
  connecting to 17, 155-159
  network forwarding 18-22
**Internet Message Access Protocol
    (IMAP) 77**
Internet of Things (IoT) service
  about 141
  dweet.io 144-147
  Freeboard 147-151
  Phant 141-144
interrupts 70-72
inVolts() function 50

IR temperature sensor
  URL 105

J

Jumper wires
  URL 7

L

Least Significant Bit First (LSB) 102
LED
  blinking 36
  fading 44, 45
  multiprocessing 37, 38
  resistor values, calculating 32, 33
  running, at startup 38
LED bar graphs
  about 80-82
  URL 80
LED displays
  7-segment displays 82
  about 77-80
  bar graphs 80
  LED matrix 85
LED matrix
  about 85-87
  URL 85
listen() method 135
Logic Supply
  URL 22
loop() function 23

M

Most Significant Bit First (MSB) 102
Mouser
  URL 6

N

network connection, BeagleBone Black
  HTTP 139
  IoT services 141
  TCP/IP 133

P

Page class 140
Phant
  about 141
  URL 141
pin multiplexing 28, 29
PIR motion detector module
  URL 88
potentiometers 72-75
pulse width modulation (PWM)
  about 4, 41-44
  Inter-Integrated Circuit (I2C) 6
  LED, fading 44, 45
  serial peripheral interface (SPI) 5
  servo motors 45-48
  universal asynchronous receiver/
    transmitter (UART) 4
PuTTY
  URL 15
PyBBIO library 23, 24
pySerial API
  URL 103

R

requests library
  URL 143
resistor values
  calculating, for LEDs 32, 33
robot
  about 55
  creating 55-57
run() function 23

S

Serial Clock (SCL) 104
serial communication 95
serial communication subsystems
  I2C 104
  SPI 110
  UART 95
serial console
  using 22, 23

Serial Data (SDA) 104
serial peripheral interface (SPI) 5, 110-114
serial port terminal emulator
  URL 23
setClockMode() method 113
setup() function 23
Simple Mail Transfer Protocol
    (SMTP) 87-89
software
  updating 23
SparkFun
  URL 6
SSH
  used, for connecting to BeagleBone
    Black 15-17
stream
  URL 141

T

ThingSpeak
  account setup, URL 156
  URL 155
through-hole soldering
  URL 83
tools and additional hardware
  about 6
  Adafruit Industries 6
  Digi-Key 6
  Farnell 7
  Mouser 6
  SparkFun 6
Transmission Control Protocol/Internet
    Protocol (TCP/IP) 133-138

U

Uniform Resource Locator (URL) 139
universal asynchronous receiver/transmitter
    (UART)
  about 4, 95-104
  pins 96
universally unique identifier (UUID) 145
user inputs
  buttons 59
  potentiometers 72

W

weather alerts
  creating 160-166
weather station
  circuit requisites 154
  creating 153, 154
World Wide Web (WWW) 139

Thank you for buying
**Learning BeagleBone
Python Programming**

About Packt Publishing

Packt, pronounced 'packed', published its first book, *Mastering phpMyAdmin for Effective MySQL Management*, in April 2004, and subsequently continued to specialize in publishing highly focused books on specific technologies and solutions.

Our books and publications share the experiences of your fellow IT professionals in adapting and customizing today's systems, applications, and frameworks. Our solution-based books give you the knowledge and power to customize the software and technologies you're using to get the job done. Packt books are more specific and less general than the IT books you have seen in the past. Our unique business model allows us to bring you more focused information, giving you more of what you need to know, and less of what you don't.

Packt is a modern yet unique publishing company that focuses on producing quality, cutting-edge books for communities of developers, administrators, and newbies alike. For more information, please visit our website at www.packtpub.com.

Writing for Packt

We welcome all inquiries from people who are interested in authoring. Book proposals should be sent to author@packtpub.com. If your book idea is still at an early stage and you would like to discuss it first before writing a formal book proposal, then please contact us; one of our commissioning editors will get in touch with you.

We're not just looking for published authors; if you have strong technical skills but no writing experience, our experienced editors can help you develop a writing career, or simply get some additional reward for your expertise.

BeagleBone Robotic Projects

ISBN: 978-1-78355-932-9   Paperback: 244 pages

Create complex and exciting robotic projects with the BeagleBone Black

1. Get to grips with robotic systems.

2. Communicate with your robot and teach it to detect and respond to its environment.

3. Develop walking, rolling, swimming, and flying robots.

Mastering BeagleBone Robotics

ISBN: 978-1-78398-890-7   Paperback: 234 pages

Master the power of the BeagleBone Black to maximize your robot-building skills and create awesome projects

1. Create complex robots to explore land, sea, and the skies.

2. Control your robots through a wireless interface, or make them autonomous and self-directed.

3. This is a step-by-step guide to advancing your robotics skills through the power of the BeagleBone.

Please check **www.PacktPub.com** for information on our titles

Learning BeagleBone

ISBN: 978-1-78398-290-5   Paperback: 206 pages

Learn how to love and care for your BeagleBone and teach it tricks

1. Develop the practical skills that are required to create an embedded Linux system using BeagleBone.

2. Use the embedded Linux software to control LEDs on the BeagleBone, empowering you to create LED flash patterns.

3. A hands-on guide, supported by practical examples to integrate BeagleBone into your projects.

BeagleBone for Secret Agents

ISBN: 978-1-78398-604-0   Paperback: 162 pages

Browse anonymously, communicate secretly, and create custom security solutions with the open source software, the BeagleBone Black, and cryptographic hardware

1. Interface with cryptographic hardware to add security to your embedded project, securing you from external threats.

2. Use and build applications with trusted anonymity and security software like Tor and GPG to defend your privacy and confidentiality.

3. Work with low level I/O on BeagleBone Black like I2C, GPIO, and serial interfaces to create custom hardware applications.

Please check **www.PacktPub.com** for information on our titles